AF264658

HIGH SCHOOL NIL

A Practical Guide to Name, Image, and Likeness in High School Sports

For Parents, Athletic Directors, and Coaches

TROY A. RUTTER

Astralight Media
PO Box 262
Ames, IA 50010

Library of Congress Cataloging-In-Publication Data
Rutter, Troy A
   High School NIL: A Practical Guide to Name, Image, and Likeness in High School Sports / Troy A. Rutter
   Paperback ISBN: 978-0-9826388-1-1
   Ebook ISBN: 978-0-9826388-7-3
   LCCN: 2026907998
   1. Sports

First Edition: June 2026
Printed in the United States of America

10 9 8 7 6 5 4 3 2 1

Contents

Introduction

The first time a parent asked me about NIL wasn't during a formal meeting or a scheduled consultation. It was after a game, in the kind of half-conversation that happens while folding up your stadium seat and kids are drifting toward the parking lot.

"Can I ask you something?" she said. "Are we supposed to be doing something about NIL by now?"

Her son was a junior and a good athlete. Not a national recruit, but competitive and still developing. They weren't looking for shortcuts or chasing headlines, they were simply trying to make sure they weren't missing something important.

What struck me wasn't the question, was the tone behind it. There was a quiet urgency there. There was a feeling that something had shifted in youth sports and that responsible families were supposed to understand it immediately.

Over the past few years, I've heard versions of that same question again and again: are we behind? Is everyone else already thinking about this? Are we supposed to have a plan already? What if we make a mistake?

The amount of information surrounding name, image, and likeness makes it difficult to separate what actually applies to high school athletes from what belongs strictly in the college conversation. Headlines focus on multi-million-dollar college deals, and social media tends to amplify the most extreme examples. At the same time, consultants and platforms promise exposure, branding, monetization, and opportunity.

Very little of it explains what matters for a family sitting in high school bleachers.

That's part of the reason ProspectBridge Sports was created.

I started ProspectBridge because too many families were being pulled into conversations that felt urgent but lacked any kind of context. Parents were told they needed highlight platforms, personal brands, recruiting exposure strategies, and now NIL plans — often all at once. What was missing in the conversation was a steady voice explaining what actually applies at each stage and what can wait.

NIL has become one of the loudest parts of that conversation. And yet, at the high school level, it is often one of the most misunderstood.

What This Book Is Designed to Do

This book is not meant to create urgency; it is meant to reduce it. It is not a blueprint for turning a high school athlete into a brand or a roadmap to endorsement income. Nor is it a shortcut to scholarships. It is a handbook for parents who want to understand the environment their young athlete is growing up in.

NIL has added a new layer to youth sports. Thia layer intersects with recruiting, school policy, eligibility rules, booster relationships, and community perception. For some, it may open modest opportunities. For others, it may never become relevant at all.

The problem is not whether NIL exists for high school athletes, it is that it is often discussed without structure. When structure is missing, parents are left trying to make decisions in a vacuum.

My role, both through ProspectBridge Sports and through this book, is not to push families toward NIL activity or away from it, but to provide context so that decisions are deliberate rather than reactive.

The Emotional Undercurrent

It's worth acknowledging something openly: most parents do not approach NIL from a place of ambition alone. They approach it from a place of protection.

They are trying to protect opportunity, preserve eligibility, and help their child avoid mistakes that could have lasting consequences. But, at the same time, they don't want to overlook something that might matter. That tension is completely understandable.

Youth sports already carry heavy emotional weight. Years of early morning and late-night practices, travel tournaments, team dynamics, school balancing acts — all of it builds toward a season, a scholarship possibility, or simply the satisfaction of personal growth. When NIL enters the picture, it can feel like an entirely new responsibility layered on top of everything else, and that can be overwhelming.

The truth: NIL does not require panic. It requires perspective.

Why Context Matters

Public conversation around NIL is shaped by college athletics, which makes sense. The legal and financial battles that led to NIL reform took place primarily at the NCAA level. Media coverage naturally focuses on the most dramatic changes and the largest financial figures.

High school athletics operate in a different ecosystem because they are governed by state associations and local school districts. They are tied to educational institutions and function inside communities where perception and precedent matter just as much as policy language.

What works at a major university does not automatically translate to a local high school program, and when families carry college-level assumptions into high school situations, confusion follows. Understanding the difference between those environments is one of the most important shifts this book will help you make.

A Word About Expectations

It is natural to be curious about the financial side of NIL. The media coverage alone makes it difficult not to wonder whether meaningful money is available at the high school level.

In most cases, opportunities, where permitted, are very modest and local. A small endorsement arrangement with a community business, a paid appearance, a youth clinic, or a limited social media promotion.

For a very small percentage of athletes, NIL may grow into something more significant over time. But for the vast majority, it will either remain small or never become central to their athletic journey or future career.

That is not discouraging. It is realistic.

When expectations are realistic, the pressure decreases and skills development remains the priority. Recruiting fundamentals remain intact. NIL becomes one potential layer of opportunity rather than the defining feature of an athlete's path.

What You Can Expect From This Book

As you move forward, this book will help you:

- Understand what NIL actually permits at the high school level
- Recognize the difference between publicity rights and pay-for-play
- Identify where authority resides in your state
- Spot situations that tend to trigger scrutiny
- Approach opportunities with calm, structured decision-making

There will be fictional scenarios drawn from patterns that occur repeatedly across states. Each story will end with a breakdown of what was handled correctly and where risk appeared. The goal is not to dramatize mistakes, but to make the invisible layers of governance visible.

There will also be a state-by-state reference section so that you can orient yourself quickly within your own jurisdiction. Policies evolve, and local interpretation matters, but having a starting point reduces guesswork.

Throughout the book, a consistent theme will emerge: clarity reduces risk.

Slowing the Conversation Down

When I speak with families, I often tell them that not every development in youth sports requires immediate action. Some require attention, others require understanding. Very few require urgency. NIL falls into the second category. It is a policy shift that should be understood, not feared and not overvalued.

If you finish this book feeling less rushed and more grounded, if you feel able to ask better questions and move deliberately rather than reactively, then it will have served its purpose.

High school athletics remain about growth, teamwork, resilience, and development. NIL does not replace those values. It simply exists alongside them, governed by rules that can be navigated responsibly.

Thanks and Acknowledgments

I want to express a very special thank you to my friend and fellow author Jim Arrowood, who helped edit and proof this book in record time. And thank you to all the parents, coaches, athletic directors, and teachers who help our young athletes grow and succeed.

How This Book Is Organized

Before we move forward, it may help to understand how the rest of this book is structured.

The goal here is not to overwhelm you with rules or turn you into a compliance officer. It is to give you a clear framework so that when questions arise — and they will — you know where to look and how to think about them.

The chapters ahead are organized in three parts.

Part I focuses on structure, scenarios and risk patterns.

We'll look at how authority is layered in high school athletics: state law, athletic associations, and local school policies, and how those layers interact. Many NIL misunderstandings begin when families assume that one layer controls everything. It rarely does.

Rather than speaking in abstract rules, we'll walk through realistic situations that families encounter: local sponsorships, social media promotions, booster involvement, transfers, school branding issues, and more. Each scenario ends with a breakdown of what was handled correctly and where risk appeared.

Part II provides a state-by-state reference guide.

Because NIL is governed at the state level, the landscape differs across the country. This section offers a concise overview of each state's general posture, common restrictions, and where to verify current guidance. It is not a legal manual, but it is designed to orient you quickly and responsibly.

Part III pulls everything together.

We'll revisit practical decision-making principles — how to ask questions early, how to document communication, how to separate NIL activity from school affiliation, and how to approach opportunities with realism rather than urgency.

Throughout the book, you'll notice a consistent theme already mentioned in the introduction: clarity reduces risk. NIL is neither something to fear nor something to chase blindly. It is a policy shift that exists within a structured system. When families understand that system, they tend to make calmer, more durable decisions.

You do not need to master every rule before turning the page, you simply need a steady framework.

That's what we'll build from here.

-Troy Rutter, May 2026.

What NIL Is (And What it is Not)

A few months ago, a parent asked me a question that I've now heard in some form dozens of times.

"Are we behind?"

Her son was a high school senior, a solid baseball player, and a good student. A couple of small colleges had shown interest. Nothing dramatic, but enough that the family felt like things were moving.

A local business reached out about a possible social media promotion, nothing formal, just a message: "Let's talk." Within a few days, that simple message had turned into a wave of uncertainty.

- Do we need to set up a company?
- Will this affect eligibility?
- Is this how recruiting works now?
- What if we wait too long?

The anxiety wasn't about the offer itself; it was about not understanding the environment.

That's usually where the confusion around NIL begins.

The Noise Around NIL

If you type "NIL" into a search engine, you'll see headlines about college quarterbacks signing six-figure deals, booster collectives raising millions of dollars, and national brands partnering with top recruits.

That's the version of NIL most people are familiar with.

It's loud, dramatic, and it makes it feel like something massive is happening and that if you don't understand it immediately, you're going to fall behind.

Here's the truth: high school NIL is different.

Before we talk about what families can or cannot do, we need to correct the mental picture many parents carry into the conversation. Because if the mental model is wrong, every decision that follows becomes harder.

So, before we talk about rules or opportunities, we need a clear definition.

What NIL Actually Means

At its simplest level, NIL refers to a person's ability to control and potentially profit from the commercial use of their name, image, or likeness.

That concept didn't begin with high school athletes. It existed way before with college sports, public figures, actors, etc.

What changed in recent years was that restrictions placed on student-athletes — particularly at the college level — were loosened. The acronym "NIL" became shorthand for that shift.

For high school athletes, NIL generally means this:

In states where it is permitted, a student-athlete can take part in situations using their personal brand, as long as those activities comply with state law, athletic association rules, and local school policies.

NIL is not a single rule. It sits inside multiple layers of authority. Even when it is permitted, it is rarely unrestricted.

At the high school level, those layers usually include:

- State law (in some states)
- The state high school athletic association
- Local school district policy
- School-level administrative oversight

When families miss one of those layers, confusion follows.

Why NIL Exists And Why That Context Matters

Understanding the origin of NIL helps lower the temperature around it.

The modern NIL shift grew out of debates at the college level. Student-athletes were generating visibility and, in some cases, significant revenue for institutions and media partners, yet they were restricted from monetizing even modest uses of their identity. Over time, policy and legal challenges reshaped that landscape.

But those changes were not written specifically with high school athletics in mind.

High school sports are not revenue engines; they are educational programs. They operate within communities, under school boards, with administrators whose primary responsibility is protecting student eligibility and maintaining competitive balance. That difference in purpose changes how NIL functions in practice.

When families assume that high school NIL mirrors college NIL, they import monetary expectations that do not align with reality.

High School NIL Is Structurally Different from College NIL

Much of the confusion families experience comes from mixing these two environments together.

College NIL frequently intersects with:

- Booster collectives organized around specific universities
- Conference-level revenue considerations
- National recruiting competition
- Media markets with substantial visibility

High school NIL operates in an ecosystem shaped by athletic associations, school administrators, and community perception.

Amateur Eligibility Frameworks

The scale of high school NIL is smaller, and the oversight is more local. The scrutiny often comes from within the same community the athlete lives in.

As mentioned earlier, for most high school athletes, NIL activity, where permitted, is modest and localized. A local restaurant promotion, a training facility partnership, a small social media endorsement, a youth clinic, etc.

Those activities may be valuable and meaningful, but they are not the same as the multi-layered financial arrangements that dominate national headlines. Recognizing that difference early prevents overcorrection in either direction.

What If NIL Is Not Permitted in Your State?

Not every state permits high school NIL activity in the same way. Some states allow it broadly under association guidance. Others restrict or prohibit certain forms of compensation. Some have adopted policies but left significant discretion to districts.

If NIL is not permitted in your state, or is heavily restricted, that does not mean your athlete is disadvantaged. It simply means the governance structure in your state has made a policy choice.

High school athletics are not uniform across the country. Eligibility rules, transfer policies, and amateur standards vary by jurisdiction. NIL is one more area where state-level decision-making matters.

If you are in a state that restricts NIL activity:

- Focus on development and fundamentals.
- Avoid informal arrangements.
- Understand that policy evolves over time.
- Start laying a foundation for when it is allowed.

The absence of NIL permission does not prevent athletic opportunity. Recruiting decisions continue to center on performance, academics, and fit — not endorsement activity. In fact, in states where NIL is not permitted, families often experience less confusion because the rules are clearer.

Clarity is not a disadvantage.

NIL Is Not Pay-for-Play

One of the most important distinctions to understand early is the difference between NIL and pay-for-play. Pay-for-play means compensation directly tied to athletic performance, team participation, or enrollment decisions.

Examples might include:

- Payment for scoring points
- Payment for committing to a particular school
- Payment for remaining at the current school
- Compensation based on wins or statistics

At the high school level, pay-for-play remains prohibited almost everywhere. NIL compensation, where permitted, must be tied to publicity value, not performance. This distinction protects competitive balance and the educational nature of high school sports.

NIL Is Not Employment

We also need to talk about a quieter concern: employment status.

NIL does not transform a high school athlete into an employee of their school or create a salary relationship or change the educational foundation of school athletics. NIL activities are generally independent arrangements between the athlete (with parental involvement) and a third party. That independence is not accidental. It is central to how high school NIL is structured.

Once NIL activity appears intertwined with school endorsement, team promotion, or institutional marketing, it becomes more complicated.

The Money Question: Realistic Expectations

It's natural for families to wonder about financial impact. The honest answer is that most high school NIL activity, where it exists, involves modest compensation. Small endorsement agreements. Limited appearance fees. Discounted services. Occasional promotional arrangements.

The overwhelming majority of high school athletes will not experience large-scale earnings. This is not a reflection of talent; it is a reflection of market economics.

Businesses compensate athletes for visibility and audience reach. Most high school athletes operate within local markets. That can still create opportunity, but it rarely resembles national headline numbers.

Talent and Market Value Are Not the Same

This is one of the most misunderstood aspects of NIL: a talented athlete is not automatically a marketable athlete. Those are two different things.

For instance: A quietly excellent cross-country runner may be one of the best athletes in the school and still attract no NIL interest at all. That does not mean the athlete lacks talent. It means there may be no obvious business reason for a local company to pay for promotion.

Or a well-known quarterback, volleyball player, or wrestler with a strong local following, a good reputation in the community, and an active social presence may be more attractive to a local business, even if that athlete is not a major college recruit.

That difference matters because families often assume NIL tracks directly with athletic level. It does not. Recruiting and NIL overlap sometimes, but they are not the same system. Coaches evaluate performance and projection. Businesses care about visibility, familiarity, and whether the athlete can help them reach actual customers.

The Myth of the Shortcut

Some families quietly hope that NIL activity will accelerate recruiting exposure. In reality, college coaches evaluate athletic performance, development trajectory, academic standing, and positional need. NIL involvement rarely alters that calculus at the high school level.

In some cases, poorly structured NIL activity can even introduce questions that complicate recruiting conversations. NIL is not a substitute for development. It is not a signal that an athlete has "made it." It is a separate layer that must be managed responsibly.

A More Stable Way to Think About NIL

When NIL is approached with urgency and fear of missing out, families tend to move quickly and sometimes without full context.

When NIL is approached as structured permission within layered governance, families move differently.

They ask:

- Who governs this in our state?
- What does our athletic association require?
- Does our district have disclosure procedures?
- Is this clearly independent of team participation?

Those questions create stability, and stability protects eligibility.

We will explore those governance layers in detail in the chapters ahead. For now, the most important shift is conceptual.

Remember, NIL is not a race. It is an opportunity that may or may not be relevant in your athlete's journey.

Parent Takeaway

NIL allows student-athletes to engage in certain commercial activities, but it does not guarantee income, nor does it replace recruiting fundamentals. If you begin with that understanding, the rest of this book will feel less overwhelming and far more manageable.

The Layers of Authority: Who Actually Decides?

FILM ROOM

Ethan's parents didn't feel reckless when they signed the agreement, in fact they felt responsible.

They had talked it through at the kitchen table the night before. The nutrition shop was locally owned. The owner had been coming to games for years and had a good reputation in town. The arrangement wasn't complicated: a couple of social media posts per month, a discount code, and modest compensation spread across the season. No incentives, bonuses, or promises. It didn't even feel like "business" so much as a friendly partnership.

His parents did what many families do when NIL enters the picture: they tried to be careful without making it a whole production. Ethan's mom pulled up the state athletic association website and searched "NIL." There it was, guidance indicating NIL activity was permitted. Ethan's dad skimmed an article that said high school athletes in their state could earn money from endorsements now. They felt a small sense of relief and moved forward.

In their minds, the "rules question" had been answered.

A week later, the athletic director asked Ethan to stop by his office.

The conversation wasn't hostile or a lecture. The AD didn't accuse Ethan of doing anything unethical. But there was a seriousness to it that Ethan could feel immediately, even before anyone said the word "eligibility."

The AD explained that while NIL was permitted under the state association's guidance, the school district required disclosure before an agreement was signed. That should have been first. Next, the post itself. The photo had been taken during a team workout and the school's logo was visible on Ethan's practice gear. The caption included a line about "fueling up for the season," blurred the line between personal promotion and team affiliation.

The AD wasn't saying that the nutrition shop post was inappropriate, he was explaining that the process mattered. The post needed to come down temporarily and the agreement needed to be reviewed. The district wanted clarification before Ethan posted again.

The hardest part for the family was the confusion.

"We checked," his mother said later. "We did our homework." They had checked one layer, and assumed it was the whole system.

The Question Most Families Ask and the One They Often Miss

When NIL first appears in a household conversation, the question almost always starts the same way:

"Is it allowed?"

That's a fair question but also incomplete.

High school athletics don't operate under a single national authority the way people sometimes assume. There's no "one NIL rule" that applies everywhere. Instead, NIL lives inside a layered governance structure. In most states, it operates within at least three levels:

- State law (in some states)
- State athletic association rules
- Local district or school policies

And there is often a fourth layer that matters just as much in real life: Administrative interpretation and enforcement. There may also be a layer of child labor laws in your particular state.

Each layer influences what happens. Missing a layer doesn't always create a disaster, but it increases the likelihood of misunderstanding, especially once something is public.

At the high school level, what matters isn't just what's permitted in theory. It's what's permitted here, under these administrators, with this school's procedures.

Layer One: State Law

Some states have enacted specific laws addressing high school NIL. Those statutes tend to establish broad permission and prohibit certain conduct, especially anything resembling pay-for-play or recruiting inducements.

Even when state law exists, it rarely covers the operational details families actually trip over: disclosure timing, logo use, facility appearance, season timing, disclaimers, or how a school wants to handle the review. State law sets the boundary lines. It doesn't referee every play. That's why families can be "right" legally and still run into a local problem.

Layer Two: The State Athletic Association

The state athletic association is the most visible governance layer for most families, and for good reason. Associations handle eligibility rules and competition standards. In many states, they publish NIL guidance or add NIL language to existing amateur rules.

This is often the layer parents find first and also where parents often stop researching.

The association may indeed say NIL is permitted, but it frequently leaves meaningful discretion to schools and districts to manage the details. You'll see language like "subject to local policy," "schools may adopt additional requirements," or "district procedures apply."

That's not the association being inconsistent, it's the association acknowledging the reality that schools are responsible for implementation.

Layer Three: Local District and School Policy

This is the layer most parents don't see until it matters.

School districts have to manage liability, equity, booster pressure, community relations, conflicts among families, and consistency across sports and teams. So even in states where NIL is broadly permitted, districts often introduce procedures such as disclosure before signing, review of contracts, restrictions on school logos and uniforms, restrictions on school facilities, disclaimers and timing guidance about the best time to pursue NIL opportunities during the year.

These aren't always posted on a clean webpage titled "NIL." They may be embedded in athletic handbooks, board policy documents, or even internal procedures that get communicated through athletic departments.

To a parent, that can feel like a hidden rulebook. To a school district, it's basic risk management.

Layer Four: Administrative Interpretation

Even written policies require interpretation. Athletic directors and administrators have to apply general rules to specific situations, often quickly, and often under pressure from multiple directions.

If an athlete posts sponsored content while wearing school gear, the administrator needs to decide whether it implies school endorsement. If a booster introduces an athlete to a business opportunity, the administrator has to decide whether that creates an improper-benefit concern.

If an arrangement becomes public at a sensitive time—during a transfer, during playoffs, or during signing season, the administrator has to decide how it will be perceived and whether documentation exists. Most administrators aren't trying to stop opportunities, they're trying to prevent situations that pull the school into disputes, complaints, and accusations of unfair advantage.

When Layers Seem to Disagree

Parents sometimes experience these layers as "mixed messages." In one place they may read state law saying NIL is allowed. The athletic association may even say it is. But then the district might add extra steps or restrictions. That can feel like a contradiction. In most cases, it's nested authority.

Broad permission at the state level doesn't automatically translate into "no local procedures." It simply means the opportunity exists inside a system that still values consistency and institutional boundaries.

A useful comparison is driving. Your state permits you to drive. Local ordinances still control speed limits, parking rules, and school-zone restrictions. Permission doesn't eliminate regulation; it just sets the framework.

A Different Outcome: What Proactive Looks Like

FILM ROOM

Maria is a junior basketball player. A local training facility contacts her about promoting their summer camps. The offer is simple: two posts, a small fee, and a discount for younger kids who register.

Maria's parents are interested, but they've heard stories about how "simple" becomes complicated if the process is skipped. Before they respond, they send a short email to the athletic director:

"Hi, Maria has been approached about a small NIL opportunity with a local business (social media promotion for a summer camp). We want to make sure we follow any district procedures. Are there disclosure requirements or restrictions we should review before moving forward?"

The email isn't defensive, asking for special permission, or trying to argue policy.

Two days later, the athletic director replies with clear guidance:

- Disclose the agreement before signing.
- Avoid school logos and uniforms in promotional content.
- Do not film inside school facilities unless rented through standard procedures.
- Include a brief disclaimer that the promotion is not affiliated with the school.

Maria's parents adjust the deal accordingly. They take photos at a public park. They keep the posts clean and personal. They submit the disclosure form. The athletic director gives a quick confirmation: "Looks fine, thanks for checking first."

The campaign runs smoothly with no complaints or awkward meetings. The opportunity isn't dramatically different from Ethan's. The difference is that Maria's family treated NIL like a structured process, not a yes-or-no rule.

A Gray Area Example: Not Wrong, Not Clean

Here's where families often get surprised: sometimes the issue isn't legality, it's how it appears.

FILM ROOM

Liam, a senior soccer player, rents the school gym for a private clinic. He does it the right way, pays the fee, signs the rental agreement, follows the rules for public use. The clinic itself is permitted. No pay-for-play concerns. No booster involvement.

But a parent takes photos and posts them online. School banners are visible in the background. Someone comments, "Nice that the school is supporting his business."

A community member emails the district asking if the clinic is school sponsored.

Now the school must respond—not because Liam did something wrong, but because the appearance of endorsement can create confusion. The resolution might be simple: add a disclaimer, avoid certain backdrops, or use a different facility next time. But it's a perfect example of why district-level procedure and administrative context matter.

High school sports operate in public view. Sometimes the problem isn't what you did; it's how it looks when it spreads.

What Athletic Directors Are Balancing

Most athletic directors are not hunting for NIL violations.

They are balancing a lot:

- Making sure one athlete's deal doesn't become another family's complaint
- Protecting the school from implied endorsements
- Keeping booster activity from turning into "benefits" territory
- Ensuring association compliance across all teams
- Responding to the community when concerns arise

When NIL shows up, the AD is often thinking in terms of precedent:

- "If we allow this, what does it invite next?"
- "If we ignore this, what complaint lands on my desk next week?"
- "If this goes public, do we have documentation?"

That mindset isn't anti-athlete, it's institutional responsibility. When families understand the athletic director's role, communication becomes easier.

Recruiting Tie-In (Without Hype)

For high school seniors bound for college, there's an additional reason to value clarity: you don't want unresolved eligibility questions hanging around during recruiting or onboarding.

Most minor NIL issues are fixable, and colleges understand that high school rules vary by state. But it's still better when a situation is clearly documented, addressed, and resolved than when it becomes a rumor or a lingering question.

This is one reason "paper trails" matter. Not because you're trying to build a legal defense, but because you're trying to avoid confusion later.

A Simple Navigation Framework

You don't need to become a NIL compliance officer. You need a repeatable process.

Here's the sequence I recommend to parents:

- Confirm state-level permission (law or association guidance).
- Find the local procedure (district handbook, AD guidance, disclosure form).

- Ask before you sign (neutral email, not a debate).
- Clarify the boundaries (logos, uniforms, facilities, timing, disclaimers).
- Keep it clearly independent (no performance-based compensation, no implied school endorsement).
- Document what you were told (save emails, keep forms).

If you do this consistently, most NIL activity becomes uneventful—in the best way.

A Template Email You Can Use

Parents often hesitate to reach out because they don't want to "raise a red flag." In practice, respectful communication usually lowers risk rather than increasing it.

Here's a simple message that works in most situations:

"Hi [Name], our student-athlete has been approached about a potential NIL opportunity with a local business. Before we move forward, we want to ensure we follow any district guidelines. Are there disclosure requirements or restrictions we should review?"

That email does three things:

- Clarifies expectations
- Demonstrates good faith
- Prevents the appearance of concealment
- Creates a documented record of compliance

Why the System Is Built This Way

It is easy, from the outside, to view layered authority as unnecessary complication. Parents sometimes wonder why there isn't one clear rulebook that answers everything in a single place.

High school programs are not separate enterprises operating independently. Athletic departments answer to school administrators. School administrators answer to district leadership. District leadership answers to school boards and communities.

Districts retain procedural control because they are the ones accountable when conflicts arise. If one athlete's arrangement causes another parent to allege unfair advantage, the complaint does not go to the state legislature. It goes to the athletic director's office.

If a promotional post appears to imply school endorsement and a business dispute follows, the district may be the one fielding questions.

Layered authority exists because responsibility is layered. Understanding that shifts the tone of the conversation. Instead of seeing district procedures as resistance, families can see them as guardrails within a system designed to prevent disputes before they escalate.

When Parents Push Back

Occasionally, a situation becomes tense not because the activity itself is improper, but because expectations differ. A parent may enter a meeting armed with printed copies of state law. They may point to association guidance that says NIL is permitted and assume that the discussion is over. From their perspective, they are advocating for their child. From the administrator's perspective, the conversation is about procedure, not permission.

This is where tone matters.

Citing state law does not eliminate district-level process. Arguing legality does not replace disclosure requirements. In most cases, the administrator is not disputing that NIL exists. They are clarifying how it must be structured locally.

Families who treat those conversations as collaborative tend to resolve them quickly. Families who treat them as confrontational sometimes create unnecessary friction. That does not mean parents should remain silent if something feels unclear. It means the framing matters. Asking, "Help me understand how this fits within district procedure," invites dialogue. Saying, "The law says we can do this," closes it.

High school athletics run on relationships as much as regulations.

Documentation Is Not Distrust

One of the most common hesitations I hear from parents is this: "If we email the athletic director and document everything, won't that make it feel like we're preparing for a fight?" In practice, documentation does the opposite.

Clear written communication protects everyone involved. It ensures that expectations are aligned before activity becomes public. It prevents misunderstandings weeks later when memories fade or staff changes.

Most administrators appreciate clarity. They prefer being informed before something circulates on social media rather than after. Documentation is not about building a defense, it is about being on the same page. When families communicate early and keep records of what they were told, eligibility questions tend to be resolved quickly because the sequence is clear.

In high school sports, clarity is often the difference between a minor correction and a prolonged review.

Why This Structure Matters Even More When Money Grows

The more visibility and money enter the picture, the more scrutiny follows. This scrutiny does not automatically imply wrongdoing; it simply reflects the reality that schools are responsible for maintaining fairness and protecting eligibility across all teams.

As we move into the next chapter, we'll explore situations where compensation intersects more directly with performance, enrollment decisions, or booster influence. In those scenarios, understanding layered authority is not just helpful, it becomes essential.

For now, the foundational shift is simple: NIL permission exists within a structure.

When families understand that structure, they are rarely surprised by how decisions are made. When more money and more outside influence enters the picture, these layers matter even more.

Pay-for-Play and Boosters

It started as a compliment.

After a Friday night football game, a well-known local business owner approached Caleb and his father near the parking lot. He had been a supporter of the program for years and always donated to the booster club.

"Great game," he said. "You've got a bright future. We should talk about ways my company can support you this season."

A few days later, the conversation became more specific. The business owner proposed a monthly payment in exchange for Caleb posting on social media and making occasional appearances at promotional events. The amount was larger than anything Caleb had previously been offered. It wasn't life-changing money, but it was significant.

Then came a sentence that made Caleb's father pause.

"We want to keep you here next year. It's good for the program."

The offer was framed as an NIL opportunity. On paper, it could even be structured that way.

But the intent mattered, and at the high school level, intent is where the line becomes clear.

The Difference Between NIL and Pay-for-Play

NIL does not permit payment for performance, playing time, or enrollment decisions. That distinction sounds simple in theory. In practice, it becomes blurry when money and influence intersect.

Pay-for-play exists when compensation is tied directly or indirectly to athletic performance or participation. That can include:

- Payment contingent on statistics or wins.
- Compensation tied to starting status or playing time.
- Offers structured around remaining at or transferring to a specific school.
- Financial benefits provided because of team membership rather than publicity value.

At the high school level, the prohibition against pay-for-play is foundational and predates NIL. It reflects a long-standing principle: school sports are educational activities, not professional contracts.

When an opportunity exists because a student-athlete has built visibility or market value, that fits. But when an arrangement exists to influence where a student plays or whether they stay, the risk escalates.

Booster Involvement: Why It Changes the Equation

Boosters are not automatically a problem. Many booster clubs operate transparently and within association guidelines. They fund equipment, travel, and program enhancements. Their support is often essential.

The problem is when booster involvement shifts from support to compensation for a player and not the program. If a booster who regularly donates to a specific sport suddenly arranges an NIL deal for one athlete, particularly one whose presence affects team success, administrators must consider whether the arrangement resembles an improper benefit. Even if the activity is labeled "NIL," perception matters.

At the high school level, booster-related compensation tied to athletic participation raises two central concerns:

- Competitive equity
- Recruiting inducement

High school associations are particularly sensitive to both.

Inducement: The Risk Most Families Underestimate

Recruiting inducement at the high school level does not look like it does in college athletics. It is often subtler. An inducement occurs when a benefit is offered to influence a student-athlete's decision to enroll, remain at, or transfer to a particular school.

Sometimes it is explicit. More often, it is implied.

- "If you stay here, we'll take care of you."
- "We want to make sure you're supported."
- "You won't get this kind of opportunity somewhere else."

Even when framed as an NIL opportunity, if compensation appears contingent on school affiliation, administrators must evaluate it carefully.

In many states, high school associations have strict rules governing transfers and benefits tied to enrollment decisions. NIL does not override those policies.

Families sometimes assume that because NIL permits compensation, it also permits influence. That is rarely the case.

A Second Scenario: When Structure Protects Everyone

FILM ROOM

Consider a different version of Caleb's situation.

A local business approaches him about promoting a summer training program. The compensation is reasonable and comparable to similar arrangements in neighboring communities. The business has no formal relationship with the school's booster club.

Caleb's family discloses the opportunity to the athletic director before signing. They clarify that compensation is based on promotional activity, not performance. They avoid linking the arrangement to team participation. The business owner avoids statements about keeping Caleb at the school.

The agreement is documented, reviewed, and it proceeds without controversy.

The presence of money did not create the issue. The link to school participation would have.

Why High School Associations Take This Seriously

High school athletics are built on competitive balance. Unlike professional leagues, there are no salary caps, revenue sharing models, or formal contracts. The system depends on trust. If families believe that team success is influenced by private compensation tied to roster decisions, confidence in fairness erodes.

That is why associations and districts respond quickly when pay-for-play concerns arise—even if the amounts involved are modest. The goal is not to suppress opportunity. It is to prevent a shift toward transactional participation.

NIL permits monetization of publicity rights. It does not convert educational athletics into open-market free agency.

Warning Signs That Require Pause

Balanced but firm means being honest about red flags. If you encounter any of the following, slow down:

- Compensation explicitly linked to staying at or transferring to a school
- Payment structured around athletic performance milestones
- A booster arranging or funding an NIL deal tied to team needs
- Pressure to keep an arrangement quiet
- Language suggesting the school expects the athlete to "represent" it commercially

These situations do not automatically create violations. But they require careful evaluation, and often legal guidance.

The Role of Intent and Documentation

Intent matters. Having proper documentation clarifies it. If an arrangement is truly based on publicity value such as audience size, community engagement, promotional effort then those factors should be reflected in the agreement.

Compensation should be reasonable relative to the activity. Excessive payments for minimal effort invite scrutiny. Clear contracts, transparent communication, and disclosure to school administrators help separate legitimate NIL from improper benefits. Secrecy does the opposite.

Why Families Sometimes Misread Booster Conversations

Boosters often speak from enthusiasm. They care deeply about programs and athletes. What sounds like encouragement can unintentionally blur into influence.

Parents may feel flattered and athletes may feel supported. Difficulties arise when support becomes conditional or transactional. A useful internal question for families is this: "If this athlete were not on this specific team, would this opportunity still exist?"

If the honest answer is no, that's a signal to slow down and evaluate structure carefully.

The Bigger Picture

At the high school level, NIL operates with guardrails designed to preserve educational priorities and competitive equity. Money does not eliminate those guardrails. In some cases, it makes them more visible.

Families who understand the difference between publicity compensation and participation compensation rarely find themselves in serious difficulty.

Those who assume the label "NIL" resolves all concerns sometimes learn otherwise. The goal is not fear. It is clarity.

When Enthusiasm Becomes Pressure

FILM ROOM

After Caleb's initial conversation with the business owner, his father replayed the exchange repeatedly in his head. On one level, it felt supportive. The business owner had invested years in the program. He had donated equipment and attended games in bad weather. His interest in Caleb seemed like another expression of community pride.

But the phrase, "We want to keep you here," lingered and introduced a subtle shift.

The opportunity was no longer just about promoting a business. It was about maintaining roster stability. That may not have been the owner's intent. Still, the implication mattered.

At the high school level, even subtle links between compensation and school affiliation can create risk.

Caleb's father decided to respond cautiously. He thanked the owner for the offer but explained that, before discussing details, they would need to consult the athletic director and ensure the arrangement aligned with district policy.

The owner hesitated. "I don't think we need to involve the school," he said. "This is just between us."

That sentence clarified everything.

Legitimate NIL activity rarely depends on avoiding transparency. When an arrangement becomes to uncomfortable to disclose, it is often because the structure may not withstand review or scrutiny.

Caleb's family ultimately declined the offer. It was not because compensation was inherently wrong. It was because the structure and intent were misaligned with the educational setting.

Walking away felt disappointing. It also felt stabilizing.

High School Is Not College

Part of the confusion around boosters stems from comparisons to college athletics. At the college level, collectives and donor-funded opportunities are widely discussed. Media coverage often highlights how alumni or supporter groups fund NIL agreements for older student-athletes. But high school athletics operate differently.

There are no formal NIL collectives sanctioned by most high school associations. There are also no scholarship negotiations tied to revenue generation. Education remains primary.

What might be normalized in a university environment can be problematic in a high school setting Families sometimes absorb college narratives and assume the same structures apply locally, but they rarely do. High school associations remain deeply protective of amateur principles. NIL may coexist with those principles, but it does not replace them.

Transfer Timing: A Sensitive Intersection

Consider a final scenario.

FILM ROOM

A sophomore basketball player transfers schools mid-year. Shortly after enrolling, he announces a new NIL partnership with a business owned by a prominent supporter of the receiving school.

The agreement may be structured as promotional activity. The compensation might be reasonable, but the timing invites scrutiny.

- Was the opportunity discussed before the transfer?
- Did it influence the enrollment decision?
- Would it have existed if the athlete remained at his previous school?
- Does the business already partner with athletes are the receiving school?

Even if the answers are clean, the review process can be uncomfortable.

This is why transparency and sequencing matter so much. If NIL discussions occur independently of enrollment decisions, the situation is easier to evaluate.

When compensation appears intertwined with transfer decisions, the risk increases.

How Gray Areas Escalate

Most serious NIL problems at the high school level do not begin with an obvious violation. They begin in a gray area.

A business owner wants to help the team and believes supporting a star athlete is the best way to do that. A parent believes their child's social media presence justifies a generous payment. A booster assumes that because NIL is "legal now," flexibility is broader than it actually is.

None of these intentions are automatically improper. The escalation usually happens in different stages.

- First, an offer is made informally.
- Second, the offer is discussed privately.
- Third, details are shaped without administrative input.
- Fourth, the arrangement becomes public.

Only then does the school learn about it. At that point, the focus shifts from structure to damage control. Administrators are no longer advising in advance; they are evaluating something that has already happened and playing clean up. That shift in timing changes tone.

When a situation is reviewed before execution, it feels procedural.

When it is reviewed after publication, it feels investigative. The activity itself may be identical. The sequence determines the stress level. This is why early disclosure protects families. It keeps gray areas from becoming reactive events.

Evaluating an Offer: A Practical Checklist

When compensation is involved, it helps to slow down and ask structured questions.

Before signing anything, consider:

- What exactly is being purchased? Is the compensation clearly tied to identifiable promotional activity: posts, appearances, endorsements? Or is it loosely framed as "support"?
- Would this opportunity exist if my child played at a different school? If the answer is no, examine the structure carefully.
- Is the compensation proportional to the activity? Excessive payment for minimal promotional effort invites scrutiny.

- Is anyone suggesting the school should not be informed? Transparency should not threaten legitimate arrangements.
- Does the agreement reference performance, statistics, or team participation? If so, it needs revision.
- Is there written documentation outlining expectations and compensation? Vague promises increase risk.

These questions should not discourage opportunities. They are meant to ensure that opportunity is rooted in publicity value rather than participation leverage.

Reasonable Compensation vs. Excessive Compensation

One of the most sensitive areas in high school NIL is determining what is "reasonable." Unlike professional sports, there is no formal market rate sheet for high school endorsements. That means context matters.

If a local business pays a modest fee comparable to what it might pay other community influencers for similar posts, the structure is easier to justify.

But if a booster-funded business pays an unusually large amount for minimal activity, particularly when the athlete's public following is limited, administrators may question whether the compensation reflects publicity value or something else.

Excessive compensation does not automatically prove wrongdoing. But it raises questions about intent. At the high school level, appearance of impropriety can trigger review even if technical violations are absent.

Keeping compensation aligned with realistic promotional value protects everyone involved.

The Subtle Pressure Families Feel

It is worth acknowledging something that rarely gets discussed openly. When compensation is offered, even modest compensation, it changes the emotional environment.

Parents may feel validated and athletes may feel recognized. Community members may frame the opportunity as proof that the athlete "deserves" support. That validation can make it harder to step back and evaluate structure objectively.

Declining an offer, especially one framed as community support, can feel like rejecting generosity. Asking for disclosure approval can feel overly cautious. Requesting formal documentation can feel like distrust. But those small hesitations are often the moments that determine whether an opportunity remains clean.

High school athletics reward patience far more often than speed.

When Saying No Is the Responsible Choice

There are times when the most responsible NIL decision is to walk away. That can be uncomfortable to admit, particularly in a culture where opportunity feels scarce and competitive.

But if an arrangement:

- Depends on secrecy
- Feels contingent on team status
- Is framed around staying at a school
- Includes unusually high compensation without clear promotional value
- Creates tension with district guidance

Declining it may protect more than accepting it.

High school careers are short. Eligibility questions can cast long shadows. Balanced decision-making does not mean avoiding NIL entirely. It means recognizing when an opportunity fits cleanly and when it does not.

Consequences: Calm but Real

It helps to approach this topic with a steady, realistic lens by neither overstating the danger nor just ignoring it. In most high school NIL situations, when something goes wrong, the outcome is usually corrective rather than punitive. Schools and state associations tend to focus on fixing the issue and restoring compliance. This might be pulling down a social media post, revising the terms of an agreement, pausing an athlete's participation while the situation is reviewed, or completing required disclosure paperwork after the fact.

More serious consequences are typically tied to more obvious violations of core eligibility principles. Problems escalate when compensation is connected directly to performance, when financial incentives influence where a student enrolls, when booster involvement crosses into improper benefits, or when families knowingly avoid disclosure requirements. Those situations are less common, but they do happen. When they do, the response is more likely to go beyond simple correction.

The purpose of this chapter is not to alarm families. It is to prevent avoidable escalation. When money intersects with school participation, scrutiny increases. That is not hostility; it is structural reality.

Connecting Back to Layered Authority

Everything in this chapter connects back to what we discussed previously about layered governance.

- State law may permit NIL
- The athletic association may outline general guidelines.
- The district must evaluate specific situations.
- The athletic director must interpret them in context.

When booster involvement, performance linkage, or enrollment influence enters the picture, those layers become more active, not less. Understanding who decides and why reduces confusion when difficult conversations occur.

Families who treat NIL as a structured privilege rather than an open marketplace rarely find themselves in serious difficulty.

Closing Reflection

NIL has changed the landscape of high school athletics, but it has not erased long-standing principles about fairness, amateur participation, and educational priority. Pay-for-play, inducements, and improper benefits are not technicalities. They are lines designed to protect the integrity of school sports.

Balanced but firm means acknowledging that compensation can exist responsibly, and recognizing that certain structures cross boundaries. The label "NIL" does not automatically make an arrangement appropriate.

Intent, structure, transparency, and independence from team participation determine whether an opportunity fits within the guardrails.

Families who understand that distinction can approach opportunities with confidence rather than fear. And confidence grounded in clarity is what protects eligibility.

School Policies, ADs, and Unseen Rules

FILM ROOM

On paper, the rules seemed simple.

Megan, a sophomore, was a highly skilled volleyball player in a state that allowed high school athletes to participate in NIL. Her mother had read a few articles, checked the state athletic association website, and found athletes could earn compensation for promoting local businesses.

A small sports facility in town approached Megan about posting two social media promotions in exchange for free private lessons and a modest payment. The offer wasn't huge or tied to her performance. It also wasn't connected to her school. It seemed harmless, maybe even educational.

Her parents asked the obvious question: "Is NIL allowed in this state?" The answer was yes, so they moved forward.

Two weeks later, the athletic director from her high school called.

The issue wasn't that Megan had signed an NIL agreement; the state allowed it. The problem was the school district had adopted its own NIL disclosure procedure that required prior notice before any promotional activity occurred. In addition, the district itself prohibited the use of phrases that connected the activity to team participation, and Megan's social media post included a line referencing her winning high school season.

No one accused her or her family of wrongdoing. But the school required the social media posts removed, the agreement revised, and future activity to be run through the athletic director. For several days, Megan was also temporarily withheld from competition while the entire situation was reviewed.

The activity itself wasn't reckless.

The Rule Structure Parents Rarely See

When families think about NIL, they usually think only in terms of legality.

- "Is it allowed in our state?"
- "If the law permits it, we're fine."

At the high school level especially, that framework is incomplete. There is another layer here that also matters: administrative interpretation and enforcement.

This means an activity technically permitted under state law may still be limited or regulated at the district level. Schools may require disclosure forms, prior approval, specific contract language, or other restrictions on how the athlete references their school affiliation. Some districts may adopt formal written policies, but others rely on handbook language or athletic department procedures.

These are not inconsistencies, they reflect the reality that high school athletics are local and not governed by a single authority. From a parent's perspective, this can feel confusing. From a school's perspective, it's risk management.

Why Schools Are Cautious

It helps to understand what an athletic director sees when NIL enters the conversation. An athletic director is responsible for:

- Maintaining competitive equity across teams
- Protecting student eligibility
- Managing booster club relationships
- Avoiding pay-for-play perceptions
- Ensuring compliance with state association rules
- Responding to parent and community concerns
- Limiting district liability

When one athlete participates in NIL activity, other families notice and ask questions. Community members form opinions. Boosters may become more active and media attention can follow.

From the school's perspective, NIL is not just about one opportunity for one athlete. It is about precedent.

Some questions an athletic director may be concerned with include if one student promotes a local business while wearing school apparel, does that create an implied endorsement from the district or school? If one athlete announces a sponsorship during signing season, does that raise concerns? If one team in the school appears to benefit disproportionately from local business partnerships, does that invite competitive complaints?

These are the kinds of issues that generate phone calls, emails, and formal inquiries.

This does not mean families must avoid NIL altogether. But it does mean approaching NIL with a "the law says it's allowed" mindset is not sufficient at the high school level.

The Gap Between "Allowed" and "Approved"

One of the most common confusions that I see is the assumption that permission flows downward. In other words: If state law allows NIL, families oftentimes assume the school must allow it as well.

In reality, schools often retain discretion over how NIL activity interacts with school property, branding, communication channels, as well as athletic participation. Some districts may require written disclosure before any NIL contract is signed. Others prohibit the use of school logos or uniforms entirely. Some may even restrict the timing of NIL promotions during the competitive season.

These local policies are not always prominently displayed or gathered in one place. They may appear in board policy minutes, athletic handbooks, or internal administrative procedures that parents do not routinely review or even have direct access to. But that does not make them irrelevant, it means they are easy to miss.

Most eligibility issues I have encountered do not begin with reckless behavior. They begin with incomplete information.

Families ask, "Is this legal? The better question to ask is, "Is this permitted?"

A Different Approach

FILM ROOM

Jordan is a junior baseball player who built a modest following on social media by posting clips and skill breakdowns as well as a few lifestyle posts. Over time, a local sporting goods store reached out and offered him a small endorsement agreement: a few paid posts and discounted equipment in exchange for tagging the store during the season.

Jordan's father had seen how easily NIL misunderstandings could escalate. Instead of responding immediately to the store to accept, he paused.

Before signing anything, he sent a short email to the athletic director:

"Hi, we've been approached about a small NIL opportunity doing social media promotion for a local business. Just wanted to confirm if the district has any disclosure requirements or restrictions we should be aware of."

The email did not address urgency, argue policy, or that state law said it was legal. It simply asked for guidance.

Within a few days, the athletic director responded and confirmed the district did allow NIL activity but required:

- Written disclosure before signing.
- Confirmation that no school logos or uniforms would be used.
- A statement clarifying that the promotion was not affiliated with the school.

- Assurance that no school facilities would appear in promotional content.

There were no prohibitions, but there were obvious boundaries.

Jordan's family adjusted the agreement with the store slightly. They also added a short disclaimer to his social media posts. They found a local field not associated with the school to film the videos. Then they submitted the required disclosure form before publishing anything.

The athletic director replied again:

"Thanks for checking on these things ahead of time. This looks fine under current district guidelines. Good luck."

The promotion ran and there were no complaints without any eligibility questions or follow-up calls. Just a successful campaign.

The opportunity did not change Jordan's recruiting possibilities. It was appropriately structured, modest, and uneventful. What Made the Difference?

The activity itself was not different from Megan's situation. Both involved local businesses. Both involved social media. Neither was tied to pay-for-play or performance incentives.

The entire difference was how it played out.

Jordan's family understood something that many families overlook: At the high school level, surprise can equal risk. Having effective communication reduces that risk.

By asking before acting, they clarified expectations, demonstrated good faith, and prevented the appearance of concealment. Athletic directors are not looking for ways to penalize families looking at NIL. In most cases, they are simply trying to prevent avoidable problems. When families bring things forward proactively, it shifts the conversation from enforcement to collaboration.

There is a difference between asking, "Can we do this?" and saying, "We've already done this."

Why This Approach Works

High school athletics run on a foundation of trust. Coaches and administrators aren't just focused on wins and losses; they're responsible for keeping their entire program within the rules. When a family shows that it's willing to work within that system, rather than around it, the tone often shifts. What might have felt like scrutiny becomes more routine oversight.

It's common for parents to hesitate, worrying that bringing something forward will create friction or invite pushback. In practice, the opposite tends to happen. When administrators are looped in early, they're in a better position to walk through the gray areas, suggest practical adjustments, and separate minor issues from more serious concerns. Just as important, they create a record that the situation was reviewed.

That early communication can matter later. If questions come up from another parent, a coach, or someone in the community, it's clear the activity wasn't hidden or handled informally. Instead, it shows a straightforward effort to do things the right way, which often carries significant weight in how the situation is evaluated.

In Jordan's case, the email exchange became a safeguard. It showed that the family sought guidance, followed district procedure, and respected boundaries. That paper trail may never be needed, but if it is, it protects the athlete.

The Larger Lesson

The safest NIL activities at the high school level are not necessarily the smallest ones. They are the ones that are transparent, structurally independent from the school, and consistent with local expectations.

Before You Move Forward

Before you move forward, a quick reminder: most NIL complications at the high school level are entirely preventable. They also do not begin with deliberate rule breaking. They begin with assumptions, often small ones, about who needs to be informed, when, and which rules apply.

Here are some quick steps before signing an agreement, posting promotional content, or accepting compensation.

Step 1: Identify All Governing Layers

Start by identifying which entities have authority over your athlete's participation:

- State law
- State high school athletic association
- Local school district policy
- Athletic department or school handbook guidelines

Do not assume that state law answers the question fully. In many states, the athletic association or school district has adopted additional procedures.

If you cannot immediately locate a written policy, that does not mean one does not exist. It may simply mean it is not prominently published.

Step 2: Review School and District Materials

Look specifically for:

- Athletic handbooks
- Board policy documents
- NIL disclosure forms
- Branding and logo usage policies
- Facility rental policies

Pay particular attention to language regarding:
- Use of school uniforms or logos
- References to school affiliation
- Timing restrictions during the season
- Required disclosure or pre-approval

If you find nothing addressing NIL directly, that is not a green light. It may indicate that the school evaluates NIL on a case-by-case basis.

Step 3: Ask Early, Ask Neutrally

If there is any question, contact the athletic director. A short, neutral inquiry works best, such as:

We've been approached about a potential NIL opportunity and want to ensure we follow any district guidelines. Are there disclosure requirements or restrictions we should review before moving forward?

This approach shows your intent to comply. Keep communication in writing whenever possible. Email exchanges provide documentation that the activity was disclosed and discussed.

Step 4: Separate NIL from the School

Before finalizing any activity:

- No school logos, uniforms, or marks are used
- No school facilities are included unless properly rented under standard public-use terms
- No coach, administrator, or school employee is organizing, promoting, or participating in the activity in their official role
- Compensation is not tied to athletic performance, playing time, or team status

If the NIL opportunity would not exist without the athlete's connection to a specific team or school, pause and reassess.

Step 5: Document What You Were Told

If an athletic director confirms that an activity is permissible, keep that communication.

Rules and administrators change. Community concerns arise days, weeks, or months after something happens. Having documentation showing that you sought guidance and received it in advance provides clarity if questions emerge later.

This is not about anticipating conflict, it is about protecting your athlete from avoidable misunderstandings.

What Triggers School Scrutiny

Schools are unlikely to scrutinize small, clearly independent NIL activity conducted transparently. They are far more likely to examine situations that appear connected to team advantage, recruiting influence, or misuse of school resources.

These examples may trigger review:

Coach Involvement

When a coach organizes, promotes, or participates in an athlete's NIL activity in their official role, it can create the appearance of school endorsement or pay-for-play. Even informal involvement such as sharing promotional materials through team channels and social media, attending the NIL event, or coordinating logistics can raise concerns.

Booster or Collective Funding

If a booster or community supporter funds an athlete's NIL opportunity, especially in connection with team participation or enrollment decisions, schools may view it as an improper benefit.

Use of School Branding or Facilities

Use of school logos, uniforms, gymnasiums, fields, or other identifiable property in promotional content can imply institutional endorsement. Even when facilities are rented properly, context matters. Promotional images that suggest school affiliation can blur boundaries quickly.

Timing During Transfers

NIL activity announced shortly before or after a transfer can attract scrutiny, particularly if the opportunity appears tied to enrollment. Schools are sensitive to recruiting inducement concerns. Timing alone does not create a violation, but it can invite review.

Public Claims Linking NIL to Team Status

Statements such as "proud to represent my school" in sponsored content may seem harmless but can create ambiguity about whether the promotion is personal or institutional. The distinction between athlete identity and school identity matters more at the high school level than many families realize.

Why Scrutiny Is Often Reactive

Schools do not typically monitor athletes' social media accounts looking for violations. A review most often begins when:

- Another parent raises a concern
- A coach receives a complaint
- A community member questions fairness
- A rival school files an inquiry

In those moments, school administrators have to respond.

Having documented disclosures and clear separation from school involvement puts you in a stronger position than those who rely solely on their interpretation of state law.

The Underlying Pattern

When NIL activity is presented in a way that feels independent, transparent, and clearly separate from school involvement, it tends to draw very little attention. Situations where the opportunity stands on its own, does not rely on school resources, and has no connection to team status or enrollment decisions are usually viewed as lower risk.

The dynamic changes when that same activity appears more closely tied to the school environment. If there are visible connections to a team, involvement from boosters, links to a transfer, or messaging that suggests the athlete is representing the school, scrutiny naturally increases. That is true even in cases where the activity itself is not prohibited.

Recognizing this pattern helps families make more informed decisions. It becomes possible to pursue NIL opportunities while still protecting eligibility, rather than feeling like the only safe option is to avoid participation altogether.

High school athletics exist within communities that place a high value on trust, fairness, and perception. Families who understand how those factors shape decision-making are far less likely to be caught off guard if questions arise.

Market Value Is Not Talent

FILM ROOM

When Tyler signed his first NIL agreement, he assumed it would reflect how good he was.

He was a senior guard averaging twenty-two points a game and led his team to back-to-back conference titles. Coaches respected him. Opponents planned around him. His family believed, reasonably, that his performance had earned attention.

A local restaurant offered him $150 to post twice on Instagram and attend a Saturday afternoon meet-and-greet.

Tyler quietly expected something bigger. He didn't say that out loud, but the number felt small compared to the hours he had spent in the gym, the travel tournaments, the early mornings, and the sacrifices.

"What's the point?" he asked his father in the car afterward. "If I'm one of the best players around, why isn't it more?"

Because market value and talent are not the same thing.

The Mental Shift Families Must Make

One of the biggest misunderstandings surrounding high school NIL is the assumption that compensation reflects athletic ability. In reality, NIL compensation reflects publicity value. That distinction matters.

A player can be the most dominant athlete in a region and still have limited NIL earning potential. Another athlete with moderate on-field impact but a strong local following may generate more opportunity. Businesses pay for attention, not statistics. At the high school level, attention is usually local. That limits scale.

What Most High School NIL Actually Looks Like

High school NIL typically looks very different from college.

In many communities, common examples include:

- $50–$300 for a sponsored social media post
- Free or discounted training sessions
- Free merchandise or equipment
- Small appearance fees at local events
- Seasonal promotional agreements valued under $1,000

These are examples, not fixed standards. Markets vary by region, sport, and visibility. But for the majority of high school athletes, NIL opportunities are modest and local. That does not make these opportunities meaningless, but it simply defines their scale.

When expectations are shaped by national headlines rather than local economics, disappointment follows.

How Local Economics Shape NIL

It helps to pause and look at this from the business side. Most high school NIL opportunities come from small or mid-sized local businesses such as restaurants, training facilities, retail stores, and service providers. These businesses operate within tight marketing budgets.

Your local restaurant is not allocating $25,000 to influencer marketing. It may have a few hundred dollars per month for promotions within the community. When that business offers $100 or $200 for a social media post, that is not a reflection of your athlete's talent. It is a reflection of that business's scale.

This is one of the most important recalibrations for families. High school NIL is usually tied to local business economics.

If the average local business spends $500–$1,500 per month on all advertising combined, a single athlete receiving a small fraction of that is realistic. Expecting four-figure monthly payments in that environment misunderstands the size of the market.

Understanding local economics protects families from comparing their situation to headlines about national brands and collegiate programs.

How Businesses Evaluate Risk

Small businesses also think in terms of risk. When partnering with a high school athlete, they are associating their brand with a minor. That introduces reputational considerations. Businesses prefer athletes who demonstrate consistency, maturity, and stability.

This is another reason why modest compensation is common at the high school level. Businesses are testing relationships.

If an athlete:

- Delivers content late
- Misses events
- Posts controversial material
- Treats the agreement casually

the partnership will likely end.

On the other hand, athletes who treat even small agreements professionally build trust. That trust may lead to expanded opportunity, not necessarily large financial increases, but sustained partnerships. Market value grows more often from reliability than from sudden attention.

Why Talent Alone Does Not Create Market Value

Let's separate two concepts:

- **Athletic Value:** How much a team benefits from your performance.
- **Market Value:** How much a business benefits from your visibility.

These are different.

When a local business looks at a potential NIL partnership, the focus is usually on reach and fit. They want to know how many people are actually seeing the athlete's content, whether those people are paying attention, will it help drive sales, and if the athlete's presence aligns with the image the business is trying to project.

Game statistics rarely drive that decision. A strong season or standout performances can help bring attention, but they are not what a business is buying. At the high school level, visibility is often tied more to audience and consistency than to performance alone, and in most cases that audience is still relatively small.

The Social Media Follower Myth

Many athletes assume that follower count equals earning power.

"I have 3,000 followers. I should be able to get deals."

But the follower count is only one variable.

Engagement rate matters more than raw numbers. A local athlete with 1,200 engaged followers in the same town as a business may be more valuable than someone with 5,000 passive followers spread across multiple states.

Businesses evaluate who is actually seeing and responding to social media posts as well as if the followers are local. For the athlete, they will look at whether they are posting content consistently and whether the athlete is relatable.

A large follower number without engagement has limited value.

Exposure Does Not Automatically Convert to Revenue

Another common misunderstanding is the belief that "exposure" equals income. An athlete may receive increased visibility such as more followers, more recognition, and more local attention without immediate financial offers Exposure can be valuable and build long-term positioning. It can also increase comfort with public engagement. But it is not a paycheck.

Businesses evaluate their return on investment. If a social media post generates minimal measurable customer activity, future offers may not increase or even continue, regardless of athletic dominance.

This is why chasing viral moments rarely produces sustainable NIL growth at the high school level.

The Resentment Problem

NIL can unintentionally introduce emotional tension inside communities and even among parents who are friends. One parent may notice another athlete received a deal and quietly wonder why their child did not.

Or a fellow athlete may assume favoritism. In most cases, the difference is not favoritism. One athlete may have built a consistent online presence for years. Another may rarely post. Or one may actively engage with local businesses while another may focus entirely on sport performance.

Neither approach is wrong, but they produce different market outcomes.

When families understand that NIL compensation reflects publicity value rather than pure talent, resentment tends to decrease.

If You Feel Behind

It is easy to compare when you see others posting content or another announcing a partnership. Social media makes visibility feel constant and competitive. This comparison can distort reality.

Many NIL arrangements are short-term, and most are modest and never renew. Public announcements of deals often exaggerate scale. If your athlete has not received opportunities, it does not mean something is wrong.

It may simply mean that their audience is still developing, their sport has limited local appeal, or that the community market is too small entirely. Silence is not failure. In fact, many athletes who focus entirely on development during high school are better positioned later when recruiting, collegiate NIL, or professional paths become more viable.

What Actually Drives High School Market Value

At the high school level, five factors typically influence NIL opportunity more than athletic dominance alone. These are audience size, engagement, brand alignment, consistency and reputation.

Notice what is not on this list: Statistical dominance. Performance can create visibility, but visibility drives compensation.

Building Market Value the Right Way

When market value is driven by visibility rather than pure athletic dominance, the next logical question becomes: Can it be developed intentionally?

The answer is yes, but be careful.

Developing market value does not mean manufacturing personality or chasing trends. It means building a consistent, authentic public presence that reflects who the athlete already is.

That might include posting game highlights alongside training clips, sharing community involvement or volunteering, demonstrating personality in a respectful way, or maintaining consistent tone and professionalism.

It does not require constant posting, but it does require thoughtful posting. Athletes who treat social media like a résumé rather than a scoreboard often see more sustainable results.

Businesses look for reliability. They want to know that when they partner with someone, the content will be delivered as promised and reflect positively on their brand. That reliability can be developed long before large opportunities appear.

When to Say "Not Yet"

Another important recalibration involves timing. Some athletes become preoccupied with monetization before they have built meaningful audience or visibility.

It is acceptable, and often wise, to decide that NIL is not a priority yet. If an athlete has fewer than several hundred local followers, limited engagement, and no consistent posting pattern, it may be more productive to focus on skill development and academic performance Market value can grow later. In fact, premature monetization can create pressure without meaningful financial return.

A Final Perspective

If NIL disappeared tomorrow, the foundations of athletic success would remain the same. People would notice work ethic, skill development, academics, character and the athlete's reputation. NIL is an addition to the landscape, not the foundation of it. Families who treat it accordingly tend to navigate it calmly.

The College Comparison

At the collegiate level, market scale is dramatically different. Games are televised. Followers on social media can reach hundreds of thousands.

Alumni networks are broader. Brand partnerships extend beyond local communities.

High school athletics rarely operate at that scale. Remember, development first, monetization second.

The most important recalibration for families is this: at the high school level, development creates opportunity more reliably than monetization does. An athlete focused primarily on maximizing short-term NIL income may neglect the very thing that increases long-term visibility: performance development.

What This Looks Like by Grade Level

Expectations should shift as athletes move through high school.

Freshman Year

At this stage, development should dominate everything. Skill growth, academic adjustment, physical maturity, and team integration matter far more than monetization. If NIL appears at all, it will likely be informal and modest. There is no urgency here. Growth compounds over time.

Sophomore Year

Visibility may begin to increase. Varsity participation, regional recognition, or improved performance may create modest local interest. This is still primarily a development phase. If small NIL opportunities arise, they should not alter training priorities.

Junior Year

Recruiting conversations often intensify here. Families sometimes feel pressure to elevate branding or expand exposure. It is critical to remember that recruiting evaluation still centers on performance, academics, and fit. NIL may exist alongside that process, but it rarely drives it.

Senior Year

Clarity increases. Offers may materialize. Future plans become more defined. NIL at this stage can be handled with greater maturity, but it still does not substitute for performance. In most cases, high school NIL remains local and limited in scope.

Across all grades, the principle remains consistent: NIL should not dictate development.

Tyler Revisited

FILM ROOM

Tyler accepted the restaurant's $150 agreement.

At first, it felt small, but he approached it professionally and delivered quality content. He arrived on time and engaged with customers at the meet-and-greet. The restaurant owner definitely noticed.

The following season, the business renewed the partnership at a slightly higher rate. Another local company reached out. None of the deals were enormous. But they were steady. More importantly, Tyler began to understand that NIL was not a scoreboard of his talent. It was a reflection of visibility and professionalism. His game continued to improve. His audience grew gradually and his reputation strengthened. Market value followed consistency, not just his performance.

Windfalls Are Rare

Large NIL payouts at the high school level are rare. They do occur in exceptional cases: nationally ranked athletes, viral personalities, highly visible recruits. But they are not the norm. For most high school athletes, NIL will supplement, not transform, their experience. When families internalize that early, they make better decisions, and they are more likely to stay focused on development.

Recalibrating the Conversation at Home

Parents play a central role in shaping expectations. If NIL becomes a measure of worth, pressure increases, but if it becomes a side opportunity that reflects professionalism and visibility, perspective improves.

Helpful reframing questions include:

- "What skills is this opportunity helping you develop?"
- "Is this building your reputation in a positive way?"
- "Does this align with your long-term goals?"
- "Would you still see value in this if no money were involved?"

When NIL is treated as an educational opportunity: learning contracts, communication, responsibility, it gains value beyond dollars.

A Realistic Earnings Spectrum

To anchor expectations, it can help to visualize the spectrum most high school athletes fall within.

At one end:

No NIL activity at all. Many athletes choose to focus entirely on sport and academics.

Next:

Occasional free gear or discounted services.

Next:

Small one-time promotional fees ($50–$250 range).

Next:

Seasonal local agreements totaling several hundred dollars.

Farther along — and much less common:

Recurring local agreements reaching low four figures annually.

Exceptional and rare:

National-level youth athletes with large sponsorship agreements.

Most families will fall somewhere in the middle of that spectrum. Understanding where your athlete realistically fits reduces emotional volatility. It prevents overreaction to modest offers and protects against discouragement when large ones do not materialize.

The goal is not to maximize position on that spectrum during high school, it is to develop the athlete so that future opportunity — athletic, academic, or professional — remains open.

Why NIL Visibility Rarely Changes Recruiting Outcomes

One of the quiet assumptions families make is that NIL activity increases recruiting visibility. It feels logical. If an athlete is posting sponsored content, gaining followers, and appearing publicly, surely college coaches will notice. In reality, recruiting evaluation operates differently. We will cover this more in-depth in Chapter 6.

The Long Game

When expectations align with reality, NIL stops feeling like a race and becomes part of the broader athletic experience, not the center of it.

High school is a developmental environment. Performance, academics, maturity, and resilience remain the core pillars of long-term success. NIL can teach communication, responsibility, and professionalism, but it should not dictate training priorities or emotional worth.

If opportunities are modest, that is normal. If opportunities are absent, that is also normal.

Market value grows from visibility and that grows from performance and character. Both take time. Families who internalize that progression approach NIL calmly. And calm families make better long-term decisions.

NIL and Recruiting

When Ava announced her NIL partnership with a regional training facility, it felt like progress.

She was a junior soccer player with solid club experience and steady improvement over the past two seasons. The training facility offered her discounted sessions and a modest promotional agreement in exchange for a handful of social media posts and two in-person appearances during the year. The money was not dramatic, but it carried weight. Her family posted the announcement on Facebook proudly and everybody shared it. Friends congratulated her.

What Ava's parents quietly assumed, though they never quite said it out loud, was that this visibility would strengthen her recruiting profile. If a business believed in her, that had to mean something. Surely college coaches would see that she was marketable, responsible, and worthy of attention.

Over the next six months, her recruiting status did not change. The coaches who were already communicating with her continued to do so. The programs that had not shown interest remained quiet. The NIL partnership neither accelerated nor damaged her recruiting path. It simply existed alongside it.

At first, that was confusing. Eventually, it became clear. Ava's family began to understand something that many families miss: NIL and recruiting operate in parallel, but they are not the same road.

A Second Story Families Recognize

FILM ROOM

Marcus's situation was different but led to the same lesson.

Marcus was a junior basketball player with strong community recognition. His parents were proactive. They created a polished recruiting profile, invested in high-quality highlight reel production, and encouraged him to build a consistent online presence.
When small NIL opportunities appeared such as, a local apparel collaboration, or a gym partnership, they treated them as part of a larger recruiting strategy.

Within months, Marcus looked impressive online. His content was clean, and his branding was consistent. Announcements created buzz. But recruiting interest did not change in proportion to that visibility.

After a season of effort, a trusted coach reviewed his film and offered direct feedback: Marcus was talented, but his competition level and role did not project cleanly to the level of schools he was targeting. The issue was not attention; it was the fit. That distinction matters more than families realize.

Recruiting is more about sorting, not a popularity contest.

How Recruiting Actually Works

From the outside, recruiting can look mysterious. Athletes appear to receive offers suddenly, and social media announcements give the impression that attention drives opportunity. Inside a college program, the process looks much more structured.

Coaches are building rosters within strict constraints. They manage scholarship limits, positional depth charts, graduation cycles, and institutional academic standards. A coach may have one scholarship available at a specific position in a given year.

When evaluating prospects, coaches typically focus on:

- In-game performance against strong competition
- Position-specific measurables and physical projection
- Tactical understanding and decision-making
- Academic eligibility
- Long-term roster fit

Marketability rarely sits near the top of that list for high school athletes. Not because coaches ignore social media entirely. They may glance at profiles or confirm identity or personality, but recruiting decisions are grounded in performance and projection.

An athlete with two local NIL partnerships is not automatically more recruitable than one with none.

Exposure Versus Evaluation

Families often assume that more visibility equals more recruiting opportunities. That may be true elsewhere, but in recruiting, this is incomplete. General exposure is not the same as targeted evaluation. College coaches discover and evaluate athletes through:

- Club and high school pipelines they trust
- Showcases and tournaments they already plan to attend
- Referrals from credible coaches
- Direct film submissions
- Ongoing tracking of known prospects

A sponsored post may increase local visibility. It rarely replaces those evaluation channels.

An athlete can build a respectable local NIL presence without it altering recruiting outcomes in either direction.

The Recruiting Timeline — With Perspective

One of the most helpful recalibrations families can make is understanding how recruiting unfolds over time. When NIL expectations are layered onto the wrong stage, confusion follows.

Elementary and Middle School

It needs to be said flat out: meaningful recruiting does not happen here for the vast majority of athletes.

There are highly publicized exceptions, especially in sports like gymnastics or basketball, but those examples distort perception. For most families, these years should focus on enjoyment, skill development, and broad athletic exposure.

The idea of a third grader signing a meaningful NIL deal may make headlines, but it is extraordinarily rare. Even when young athletes gain social media attention, that visibility is often novelty-driven and short-lived. It is not a stable market signal.

Monetization at this stage typically adds pressure without adding long-term value.

Freshman Year of High School

Recruiting awareness may begin, but decisions are rarely made this early outside of exceptional cases.

This year should prioritize skill refinement, physical development, academics and practice getting good film clips. If any opportunities do come up, they should be proportionate to this early stage.

Sophomore Year

Evaluation often becomes more serious. Coaches begin tracking trajectories. They want to see progression, not just talent, but improvement.

The most productive focus areas include:

- Stronger competition exposure
- Updated film
- Honest feedback about level
- Initial, respectful outreach

NIL visibility rarely changes evaluation at this stage. Coaches are projecting physical and tactical development, not audience growth.

Junior Year

For many sports, this is the most significant recruiting year. Offers, visits, and serious conversations are frequently concentrated here.

Time management becomes critical. Families sometimes escalate branding efforts at precisely the moment development and communication matter most.

The most effective junior-year investments include:

- Consistent performance
- Direct communication with programs
- Targeting realistic levels
- Academic readiness
- Strategic event selection

If NIL exists, it should not compromise training or communication windows.

Senior Year

By senior year, recruiting outcomes are clearer. Some athletes commit early; others find opportunities later in the cycle. NIL at this stage may provide useful experience, but it rarely reshapes recruiting trajectories dramatically.

Understanding this timeline protects families from chasing branding solutions during developmental windows.

Recruiting Myths That Intersect With NIL

When NIL entered the high school conversation, several recruiting myths quietly intensified.

Myth 1: "If my athlete builds a following, coaches will notice."

Coaches notice performance first. Social media may provide context, but it is rarely the discovery mechanism.

Myth 2: "An NIL deal proves college readiness."

Local business interest reflects community visibility. It does not guarantee competitive projection at the college level.

Myth 3: "Branding can compensate for marginal performance."

It cannot. Branding may enhance reputation once recruiting interest exists. It does not substitute for skill, size, speed, or tactical fit.

Myth 4: "If another athlete is signing deals, they must be more recruitable."

Not necessarily. Market visibility and recruiting evaluation measure different things.

Myth 5: "NIL is the new recruiting strategy."

For the vast majority of high school athletes, it is not. It is an adjacent opportunity.

What Actually Moves the Needle

If we strip away hype and focus on patterns, recruiting outcomes tend to hinge on:

- Verified performance against credible competition
- Measurable physical development appropriate to level
- Academic eligibility
- Clear, respectful communication
- Realistic targeting of program fit

These variables are not flashy, but they are consistent. When families allocate time and resources, those factors deserve priority.

The Most Underused Tool: Direct Communication

Many families invest heavily in exposure but hesitate to initiate direct contact with programs. In reality, simple, professional communication often does more than passive visibility. A concise introduction email that includes graduation year, position, film link, academic information, and schedule can open doors more effectively than a polished announcement.

Coaches respond to clarity.

NIL can teach professionalism, but recruiting still requires proactive communication.

Where NIL May Matter

There are limited circumstances where marketability intersects more visibly with recruiting, particularly for nationally ranked prospects. In those rare cases, audience scale can become part of broader institutional conversations.

Even then, performance remains foundational. Coaches recruit athletes who can compete. Marketability may enhance opportunity after commitment, not before. For most high school athletes, NIL does not determine scholarship outcomes.

Division Levels and Why Expectations Must Shift

One of the most common recruiting mistakes families make is assuming that all college levels operate the same way. They do not. Understanding this can recalibrate expectations immediately.

Division I

Division I programs operate with the greatest financial resources and media exposure. Coaches at this level often recruit nationally or internationally. They rely heavily on verified performance, scouting networks, and measurable athletic projection.

At this level, NIL may intersect with recruiting only in rare cases, typically when the athlete is already a highly ranked prospect with national recognition. For most high school athletes, NIL activity will not move them from "not a D1 recruit" to "D1 recruit." The evaluation standards are performance-based and projection-driven.

Division II

Division II programs often operate with partial scholarships and tighter recruiting budgets. Coaches prioritize athletes who fit their system and can contribute immediately or within a development window. NIL rarely factors into evaluation at this level during high school. Coaches are focused on roster balance and affordability. Strong communication, film, and realistic self-assessment matter far more than social media presence.

Division III

Division III programs do not offer athletic scholarships. Recruiting focuses heavily on academic fit, character, and roster needs.

NIL has minimal influence in high school recruiting for Division III programs. Coaches evaluate contribution and cultural fit. An athlete's professionalism online may reflect positively on maturity, but sponsorship announcements do not typically influence roster decisions.

NAIA and Junior College

NAIA and JUCO programs often recruit later in the cycle and may provide flexible opportunities for development. Coaches at this level value athletes who demonstrate readiness and work ethic.

Again, NIL visibility does not generally drive evaluation. Fit, availability, and performance remain central.

Understanding these distinctions protects families from chasing branding milestones that do not align with the level they are realistically targeting.

When NIL May Matter More: After Commitment

There is one stage where NIL and recruiting intersect more visibly: after an athlete has already committed.

Once a roster spot is secured, marketability may enhance opportunity in certain programs. College NIL environments are broader and more structured than high school environments. These happen in a distinct order: recruiting, commitment, and market opportunities. If families reverse that order, they often experience frustration.

High school NIL should not be treated as a gateway to college NIL. It may provide useful experience, learning to communicate with businesses, honor agreements, and manage time, but it does not guarantee future earnings. Performance and fit still unlock those doors.

The Recruiting Reality Check

It is uncomfortable but we need to talk about something deeper: NIL recognition feels validating.

When a business approaches an athlete, it signals belief. That validation can subtly shift family expectations. It can inflate assumptions about recruiting level. It can create pressure to match public perception with scholarship outcomes.

An athlete can be:

- Marketable locally
- Well-liked in the community
- Professional online
- Consistent in posting

and still project most realistically at a Division II, Division III, NAIA, or junior college level. There is nothing less along those paths. Recruiting success is not determined by how loudly it is announced, but by fit, opportunity, and long-term development.

When families separate ego from evaluation, decisions become clearer. NIL is not a ranking system, a recruiting ladder, or proof of division level. It is an opportunity layered onto an athlete's current visibility.

Protecting Development in the Recruiting Window

The final consideration is time, especially during junior year. Opportunities can change quickly, and college coaches evaluate athletes in waves. Even small shifts in focus can matter. When attention starts to lean more toward branding metrics than competitive performance, important evaluation windows can quietly pass.

It helps for families to check in on how that time is actually being used. If more energy is going into posting than training, if attention is drawn to announcements instead of competition, if school interest is being shaped by image rather than realistic fit, or if day-to-day preparation begins to slip, those are signals worth noticing early.

NIL opportunities can exist alongside recruiting, but they work best when they remain in a supporting role rather than taking up the space that performance and development require.

Evaluating "Momentum" Without Losing Perspective

One of the most destabilizing parts of recruiting is the silence that goes with waiting to hear from someone about one's status.

Families often assume that visible progress must accompany effort. If an athlete is hitting all they "should" be doing, it is easy to think there should be measurable response. When that does not appear quickly, doubt creeps in.

If an athlete signs a partnership and gains local recognition, families may interpret that as upward momentum. When recruiting interest does not match that energy, it can feel like something is broken. It usually isn't.

Recruiting moves in cycles that are not always visible to families. Coaches evaluate in waves. Scholarship numbers shift. Roster needs change after unexpected transfers. Budget decisions alter timelines. An athlete may simply be in the second tier of a position group, waiting for a first-tier decision to finalize.

Silence does not always mean disinterest. It often means timing. Understanding that reduces overreaction.

The Difference Between Attention and Traction

It helps to distinguish between attention and traction.

Attention looks like:

- Likes and comments
- Announcement posts
- Increased follower count

- Public congratulations
- Traction looks like:
- Coaches responding consistently
- Requests for additional film
- Invitations to campus or events
- Honest feedback about fit

Attention can exist without traction, but traction rarely exists without evaluation. NIL announcements often generate attention. Recruiting momentum depends on traction. When families confuse the two, they misinterpret signals.

Honest Level Assessment

Another hard but necessary part of this conversation involves level projection.

Families sometimes use NIL visibility as evidence that their athlete belongs at a higher division level than objective evaluation suggests. A sponsored post can feel like validation of elite status. But recruiting operates on projection, not validation.

A productive question to revisit periodically is: "If NIL did not exist, what level would this athlete realistically project to if based on performance and measurables alone?"

This question anchors expectations.

If the answer points toward Division II, Division III, NAIA, or junior college, that is not a failure. Those programs offer meaningful athletic and academic experiences. They simply operate within different competitive and scholarship structures.

NIL visibility should not inflate projection.

The Role of Ego — and How to Manage It

It is uncomfortable to discuss ego in youth sports, but it plays a role. When an athlete becomes visible, when businesses reach out, when announcements circulate, it can subtly shift identity. The athlete may begin to see themselves as already elevated. Parents may feel external pressure to match that visibility with a certain recruiting outcome. That psychological shift can influence decision-making.

Athletes may turn down realistic opportunities because they expect a "bigger" one. Families may delay committing to strong fits while waiting for prestige.

Remember, prestige does not guarantee fit. Fit sustains careers. NIL recognition should be treated as if something is working in the present, not a sign of a long career.

Protecting the Recruiting Window

Time remains the most limited resource.

Junior year, especially, is finite. Coaches make decisions based on evaluation windows families cannot always see. If development, communication, or recovery are compromised by overextended commitments, momentum can stall.

A simple guardrail families can use is this: If an NIL commitment ever causes missed training, increased fatigue during competition, or reduced responsiveness to coaches, it needs to be scaled back.

No local partnership is worth compromising the primary objective.

Bringing It Back to First Principles

When recruiting becomes complicated, it helps to return to fundamentals.

College programs are trying to answer a basic question: "Can this athlete help us win, develop, and represent our institution well?"

NIL may demonstrate responsibility. It may reflect maturity. It may signal reliability, but it does not answer the competitive question. Performance does. When families internalize that truth, NIL stops feeling like leverage and starts feeling like a supplement. That is the correct proportion at the high school level.

A Balanced but Firm Reality

When NIL and recruiting are placed in their proper order, you will notice results. Recruiting remains about development and learning, NIL is still secondary and teaches professionalism, but performance becomes the common denominator.

Families who understand this avoid overreaction and invest in development first and allow opportunity to scale naturally. That discipline does not limit potential, it protects it.

Final Perspective: Keeping NIL in Its Proper Place

By the time families reach this point in the conversation, two recalibrations should feel clearer. First, market value is not the same thing as talent. Second, NIL visibility is not the same thing as recruiting leverage.

For most high school athletes, the healthiest framework is simple: let recruiting decisions be driven by performance, development, and fit. Allow NIL to exist proportionately to current visibility, without inflating its role.

In the next chapter, we'll look more closely at visibility itself; how social media presence shapes reputation, how to build it responsibly, and how to avoid common digital mistakes that can create risk. Because while NIL does not drive recruiting for most athletes, public presence still matters.

The key is understanding what it can and cannot do and placing it accordingly.

Transfers, Inducements, and Timing

FILM ROOM

The conversation began like any other post-game exchange.

After a summer basketball tournament, Marcus and his father were walking toward the parking lot when a man they recognized from the stands approached them. He was sitting near the bench during the games and had been enthusiastic whenever Marcus made a strong play. At first it felt like any other post-game congratulations between a supporter and a family whose child had just competed well.

The man congratulated Marcus on his performance and spoke for a few minutes about the tournament. Eventually the conversation drifted toward high school basketball. He mentioned a nearby program that had recently become competitive in the region and talked about the culture of the team and the quality of the coaching staff.

Then the tone shifted slightly.

"If you ever thought about transferring there," the man said, "there are a lot of people in the community who like to support our players."

Marcus's father listened but didn't respond immediately.

"Local businesses are starting to work with athletes now that NIL is a thing. Our town has really embraced it."

Nothing in the conversation sounded overtly improper. No money was mentioned and no agreement was proposed. Yet the implication lingered in the air long after the conversation ended.

Marcus's father drove home that night thinking about what had just happened. On the surface it sounded like encouragement. Underneath it sounded like something else, like the possibility financial opportunity might be connected to where his son played.

That subtle distinction is exactly where NIL and high school athletics become complicated.

Why Transfers Draw Attention

Transfers have always been part of high school sports. Families move for jobs, housing, and academic opportunities. Athletic associations understand this mobility is part of life, and most states have established policies designed to handle these situations fairly.

At the same time, high school sports were never designed to function like professional leagues where players move between teams based on competitive advantage. Schools compete within a structure that emphasizes community identity, educational purpose, and reasonable competitive balance. Transfer rules exist largely to preserve those values.

Because of that, athletic associations tend to examine transfers carefully, particularly when the move appears connected to athletic participation. Before NIL existed, administrators already evaluated situations where families relocated shortly before a season began or where talented athletes appeared at programs with strong competitive reputations. NIL has added another dimension.

When money enters the conversation, even indirectly, administrators must determine whether the financial opportunity is connected to publicity value or whether it is functioning as an incentive tied to school enrollment.

That question is where the concept of inducement becomes important.

Understanding Inducements

In the language of high school athletics, an inducement is something of value offered to influence where a student enrolls or remains enrolled. The definition is intentionally broad because inducements can and do take many forms.

Historically, inducements might have involved free housing arrangements, transportation assistance, job opportunities for parents, or direct financial benefits offered to families whose children could help a program succeed competitively. Athletic associations created rules to prevent those practices because they undermine the idea that high school sports should reflect school communities rather than recruiting markets.

NIL introduces a new variable. Instead of direct payments tied to participation, businesses may now compensate athletes for promotional activity connected to their public identity.

In theory, those two ideas are separate. NIL compensates publicity value and inducements influence enrollment. In practice though, the line between the two can become blurry if families are not careful.

If a business suggests that NIL opportunities would exist specifically because an athlete attends a certain school, the conversation begins to resemble an inducement rather than a partnership. Even if no formal agreement is made, the suggestion itself can create questions about whether enrollment decisions are being influenced by financial incentives.

For administrators responsible for protecting competitive fairness, those questions cannot be ignored.

Timing Creates Questions

Timing is often what draws attention to potential inducement issues. Imagine a scenario in which an athlete transfers schools during the offseason and announces a new NIL partnership shortly afterward with a business owned by a prominent supporter of the receiving program. Even if the agreement is legitimate and involves real promotional work, the particular sequence of events can raise concerns.

Administrators need to determine whether the NIL opportunity was discussed before the transfer occurred or whether it played any role in the decision to move schools. They also look at whether the arrangement would have existed regardless of where the athlete enrolled.

None of those questions automatically lead to penalties or violations for the athlete. However, they do trigger review processes that can temporarily affect eligibility while the situation is evaluated.

Families sometimes assume that if an NIL agreement complies with state law, the surrounding circumstances are irrelevant. High school athletics operate within a layered governance structure that includes state law, athletic association policies, and local school rules. Even legal NIL activity can create complications if the context suggests that enrollment decisions were influenced by financial opportunity.

Understanding that dynamic helps families approach NIL thoughtfully rather than reactively.

Booster Influence and Community Enthusiasm

Community support is one of the defining characteristics of high school athletics. Booster clubs organize fundraising events, businesses sponsor scoreboards and uniforms, and local supporters often take pride in the success of school teams. These contributions are generally positive and help sustain programs that operate with limited budgets.

The challenge arises when enthusiastic supporters begin focusing their energy on individual athletes rather than the program as a whole.

Boosters sometimes believe they are helping by introducing athletes to business owners who might be interested in NIL partnerships. In many cases, their intentions are sincere. They simply want to reward talented players or encourage them to remain in the community.

Unfortunately, good intentions do not eliminate compliance concerns. When boosters appear to be arranging NIL opportunities tied to a particular program, the perception can shift from community support to recruiting influence.

Athletic directors understand this risk well. That is why responsible administrators often discourage boosters from playing active roles in connecting athletes with sponsors. Even casual conversations can create misunderstandings if they imply that NIL opportunities depend on school affiliation.

For families navigating NIL for the first time, recognizing the sensitivity around booster involvement is essential.

Fred, a sophomore quarterback, receives attention after a strong playoff run. During the offseason, a local business owner who regularly donates to the football booster club approaches his family and suggests that several businesses in town would be willing to sponsor him through NIL arrangements.

At first the idea sounds flattering. The business owner explains that the community wants to "take care of the kids who represent the school well." The conversation continues over several weeks and eventually includes references to the upcoming season and how valuable he will be to the team's success.

From the family's perspective, the discussion feels like community appreciation. From an administrator's perspective, the conversation raises concerns. The NIL opportunity appears connected to the athlete's role within a specific program rather than to independent publicity value.

The safest outcome in situations like this is usually to pause the conversation and involve the athletic director before any agreements are discussed further. Early transparency often prevents small misunderstandings from becoming formal compliance reviews.

Communication as Protection

One of the most effective ways families can protect their athletes during NIL conversations is through proactive communication with school administrators. Athletic directors are accustomed to interpreting policies and advising families on how to avoid potential problems.

When NIL opportunities appear near the time of a transfer, informing the athletic director early allows the school to evaluate whether the arrangement appears independent of enrollment decisions. In many cases administrators can simply document that the opportunity originated outside the school environment and confirm it aligns with association guidelines.

Waiting until an agreement becomes public makes the situation more difficult. At that point administrators must respond to questions from other schools, community members, or association officials without having had the opportunity to review the arrangement beforehand. Transparency shifts the process from investigation to collaboration.

FILM ROOM

Kate, a junior soccer player, receives an NIL inquiry from a regional training facility that wants her to promote youth camps on social media. Around the same time, her family is considering transferring to another school because it offers an academic program that better fits her interests.

Recognizing the potential sensitivity, the family contacts the athletic director at the new school before finalizing anything. They explain the origin of the NIL opportunity, provide documentation of the promotional work requested by the training facility, and clarify that the business operates independently from the school's booster community.

After reviewing the information, the athletic director confirms the arrangement appears unrelated to the transfer decision and advises the family to keep records of the agreement and promotional activity.

Because the family addressed the situation early, the NIL opportunity proceeds without controversy and the athlete maintains full eligibility. The key difference was not the presence of NIL. It was the structure and transparency surrounding the decision.

Keeping the Purpose of NIL in Perspective

High school NIL was designed to allow student-athletes to benefit modestly from their public identity without turning school sports into professional marketplaces. That balance depends on maintaining a clear separation between publicity value and enrollment decisions.

When NIL opportunities arise because an athlete has built a reputation through performance, community engagement, or social media visibility, they generally align with the intended purpose of the policy. When the opportunity appears to exist primarily because of the athlete's relationship to a particular team or school, administrators must examine the situation more carefully.

Families who understand that distinction rarely find themselves in difficult situations. They approach NIL opportunities with patience and transparency rather than rushing to finalize agreements.

The goal is not to eliminate opportunity, it is to ensure opportunity develops in ways that respect the structure of educational athletics.

Trusting Your Gut

Parents often ask a practical question at this point: How do we know if we're getting close to a problem?

The answer is not always obvious, because inducement situations rarely appear in dramatic or obvious ways. They often begin with casual conversations that feel supportive or flattering. Someone in the community expresses enthusiasm about a player's future. A business owner mentions how much they enjoy watching the athlete compete. A booster casually notes that local companies enjoy supporting the program.

None of those comments are violations by themselves. High school sports communities thrive on encouragement and pride. The difficulty arises when those conversations begin to suggest financial opportunities might depend on where an athlete enrolls.

When families hear comments like that, the safest approach is to slow the process down and ask a few grounding questions.

- Would the business still want to work with my child if they attended a different school?
- Was the opportunity introduced independently of any school program or booster network?
- Is the compensation tied clearly to identifiable promotional activity rather than to participation in a particular team?

If those answers remain clear and consistent, the opportunity is far more likely to fall within the intended purpose of NIL. If the answers become vague or uncomfortable, it is usually a signal the situation deserves a pause and possibly a conversation with the athletic director.

Families sometimes hesitate to involve administrators because they worry it could create resistance or cause the opportunity to disappear. In reality, the opposite is often true. Athletic directors prefer to address questions early, when small adjustments can prevent misunderstandings later.

Waiting until a deal becomes public can place administrators in a difficult position. At that point they must respond to questions from other schools, association officials, and community members without having had the chance to review the arrangement beforehand. Even a perfectly legitimate deal can create unnecessary stress if it appears suddenly without context.

Another concept families should understand is what administrators sometimes call an "accidental inducement."

An accidental inducement occurs when a well-meaning supporter unintentionally frames an opportunity in a way that links financial benefits to school participation. The person making the comment may not realize the implication of their words.

A booster might say something like, "If you come play here, businesses in town will really take care of you."

From the booster's perspective, the statement may simply be enthusiasm. From an administrator's perspective, it creates the appearance that financial incentives are tied to enrollment. Most of these situations never develop into formal arrangements, but they illustrate how easily misunderstandings can arise when NIL conversations intersect with school identity.

The safest response to those moments is not confrontation. It is clarity. Parents can respond calmly by explaining that any NIL opportunities would need to remain independent of school affiliation and would likely require disclosure to school administrators. Such a response usually redirects the conversation back to a safer place.

At the same time, it is important to recognize that many transfers occur for completely legitimate reasons having nothing to do with athletics or NIL. Families relocate for employment opportunities. Students seek academic programs that better match their interests. Transportation logistics, family circumstances, or personal wellbeing sometimes make a different school environment more appropriate.

Athletic associations understand that reality, and most transfer policies include provisions allowing eligibility when a move is clearly connected to educational or family considerations.

When NIL enters the picture during those situations, families simply need to be mindful of how the opportunity is structured. If the promotional agreement originates independently and would exist regardless of school enrollment, the arrangement is far less likely to trigger compliance concerns.

In other words, legitimate transfers and legitimate NIL opportunities can coexist. The key is to ensure the two decisions are not influencing each other.

One-way families can protect themselves is by documenting the timeline of events. If a transfer decision occurs first and an NIL opportunity appears later through independent outreach, that sequence helps demonstrate the two situations are unrelated.

Similarly, if a business contacts an athlete based on social media visibility or tournament performance, keeping records of those communications can provide helpful context if questions arise later.

Documentation does not mean families should treat every conversation like a legal proceeding. It simply means maintaining enough clarity that the story of how an opportunity developed remains easy to explain.

Another helpful practice is to avoid announcing NIL agreements immediately after a transfer becomes official. Even when everything has been handled appropriately, sudden public announcements can create the appearance of coordination between the move and the financial opportunity.

Allowing some time to pass before promoting new partnerships can reduce unnecessary speculation and give administrators confidence that the arrangement developed independently.

For most families, these situations will never arise. The vast majority of high school athletes will never experience transfer-related NIL questions because their opportunities develop naturally within their existing school environments.

Still, understanding the issue matters because it reinforces a broader principle that runs throughout high school athletics.

Educational sports programs operate on trust. Schools trust families to act in good faith and families trust schools to treat their children fairly. Communities also trust competition reflects the efforts of students rather than the financial influence of outside supporters.

When NIL opportunities grow from an athlete's reputation, character, and visibility rather than from enrollment decisions, trust remains intact. And when families approach opportunities thoughtfully, they rarely encounter the complications that sometimes dominate headlines about NIL and recruiting.

Closing Perspective

Marcus eventually received legitimate NIL opportunities during his high school career. They came from businesses that appreciated his visibility in the community and wanted to connect with young athletes following his social media accounts. None of those opportunities depended on which school he attended.

Looking back, Marcus's father was grateful he had paused after parking lot conversation. The momentary hesitation gave him time to recognize the difference between encouragement and influence.

When NIL opportunities grow naturally from an athlete's visibility and character, they can provide valuable learning experiences and perhaps, modest financial rewards. When opportunities become intertwined with recruiting conversations or transfer decisions, they create risks few families anticipate.

Understanding boundaries allow families to move forward with confidence, knowing that opportunity and eligibility can exist side by side when the structure remains clear.

Development First: Why Performance Still Wins

The temptation to accelerate is understandable.

When NIL becomes part of the conversation, it introduces a subtle pressure to look established before the athlete is fully developed. Social media rewards visibility. Sponsorship conversations reward polish. Public announcements reward momentum.

Development, however, rewards patience. Those two timelines do not always move at the same speed.

FILM ROOM

Dan, a sophomore basketball player, begins to attract modest local attention. A small apparel brand sends free gear and a training facility offers discounted sessions in exchange for promotion. His online presence grows.

What begins to change, almost imperceptibly, is how he allocates his time.

He starts filming workouts instead of finishing them. He edits highlight clips late into the night. He tracks follower growth during class breaks. None of these decisions feel dramatic. They are small reallocations of energy.

But his lift numbers plateau. His defensive footwork stops improving. His conditioning dips slightly late in games. Nothing catastrophic happens, he has simply stalled.

When his parents looked at his schedule, the solution was obvious. They moved training back to priority and content became secondary. Sleep improved. Within a season, development resumed. NIL had not harmed him, misplaced priority had.

The Long Arc of Athletic Development

High school athletics exist within a narrow window. The body, however, develops over a much longer arc.

From a physical standpoint, most athletes are still building strength, power, speed, neuromuscular coordination, endurance and recovery capacity. These adaptations do not respond well to inconsistency. Performance gains require muscle overload, sufficient rest, and disciplined repetition. Social media metrics do not measure those variables. Cameras do not accelerate them.

When families shift attention toward presentation too early, they sometimes sacrifice the quiet work that produces durable performance. The irony is simple: athletes who remain most disciplined in development often become the most marketable later.

Not because they chased branding, but because they became undeniably good.

Skill Before Spotlight

In sports, technical skills take years to refine.

- Footwork in soccer
- Pitch sequencing in baseball
- etc.

These are not mastered through exposure. They are mastered through repetition and correction.

If NIL commitments begin to interrupt skill sessions, the long-term cost can exceed the short-term benefit. That does not mean athletes cannot balance both, but families need to be vigilant.

Ask a simple question regularly: "Are we improving?"

If the honest answer is no, rebalance.

Strength and Recovery: The Invisible Advantage

Parents often underestimate how much performance at the next level depends on physical preparation. College coaches consistently report that one of the largest gaps between high school and college athletics is strength and recovery capacity.

Athletes who prioritize consistent lifting, nutrition, hydration, sleep and injury prevention separate themselves quietly. These habits do not trend online, but they do win games.

If an NIL commitment pushes bedtime later or compresses recovery windows during season, the trade-off deserves reconsideration. At the high school level, development time compounds. Small improvements can lead to meaningful strides by senior year.

Academics Are Not Separate From Development

It is tempting to separate athletic ability from academic performance. However, eligibility, admissions, and institutional fit all intersect with academics. An athlete who manages time effectively, maintains grades, and communicates responsibly signals maturity. An athlete who manages time effectively, maintains grades, and communicates responsibly signals maturity.

NIL activity can reinforce those habits or erode them. If an athlete begins to prioritize promotional deadlines over academic responsibilities, recalibration is necessary. Professionalism begins in the classroom.

Identity and Pressure

There is another dimension to development that rarely gets discussed openly. When an athlete becomes visible, identity shifts. They are no longer just a teammate. They are "the athlete with deals." That subtle distinction can change how peers respond and how the athlete sees themselves.

If identity becomes tied to visibility rather than growth, development may slow.

Athletes who remain internally motivated, who see NIL as an accessory rather than a definition, tend to sustain progress.

Parents play a crucial role here. Reinforce effort, not announcements. Celebrate improvement, not partnerships. Keep praise anchored to work ethic.

Early Specialization and Burnout

NIL may unintentionally accelerate specialization.

If a young athlete begins receiving sport-specific promotional opportunities, families may feel pressure to double down early. Multi-sport participation may shrink. Off seasons may disappear. Research and long-term coaching experience consistently show that diversified sports often enhance long-term performance and reduce burnout.

High school careers are short and burnout is real. If NIL activity intensifies training volume beyond sustainable limits, reassess. Long-term development often benefits from seasonal balance.

What a "Development First" Week Looks Like

It helps to visualize proportion. A balanced in-season week for a high school athlete might include:

- 4–5 team practices
- 1–2 strength sessions
- Academic workload
- Recovery time
- Family/personal time

If NIL content creation adds 6–8 additional hours, this schedule compresses.

A healthier structure might look like:

- 1 planned content session per week
- Batch filming during off-season
- Limited appearance commitments during season
- Defined "no phone" recovery windows

Having this structure protects performance.

The College Perspective

College coaches are evaluating trajectory. They want to see the athlete's year-over-year improvement and resilience.

A junior who improved strength, sharpened skill, and demonstrated maturity often projects more favorably than one who plateaued while maintaining strong online presence.

Recruiting still begins with performance. NIL does not reverse that hierarchy.

The Athlete Who Quietly Progresses

Consider a cross-country runner who has minimal online presence and no NIL partnerships during her first two years of high school. She focuses relentlessly on incremental improvement. Her times improve, her strength increases, and she manages academics carefully.

By junior year, she attracts recruiting interest organically. A local running store approaches her about modest promotion. She accepts.

Her NIL presence emerged after her performance established credibility. Her skills development created the opportunity, not the other way around.

Scaling Without Losing the Center

When athletes do begin to experience traction, returning to first principles becomes essential. Before adding a new partnership, ask:

- Will this interfere with training cycles?
- Does it require in-season travel?
- Does it increase stress?
- Is compensation proportional to time invested?

Scaling should feel sustainable, not frantic. If anxiety increases with opportunity, something may be misaligned.

Long-Term Thinking

High school NIL may feel urgent in the moment. It rarely defines long-term trajectory. Habits formed during high school will.

Athletes who learn to:

- Manage time
- Prioritize recovery
- Handle modest income responsibly
- Communicate professionally

will be able carry those habits forward in their lives. The spotlight may fade, but the discipline remains.

A Case Study in Burnout

FILM ROOM

Joy, a sophomore soccer player, began attracting attention early. Her freshman year was strong, she made varsity and gained local recognition. A regional training brand reached out about social media collaboration. Nothing inappropriate or excessive.

By mid-sophomore year, she was training year-round with no true off-season. Club season overlapped with high school conditioning. Promotional filming filled the gaps between sessions.

Her weekly schedule looked like this:

- 5 team practices
- 2 club training sessions
- 2 strength sessions
- Weekend tournament travel
- 3 sponsored content filming blocks
- Academic workload

On paper, she was "busy but driven," but in reality, her body was under-recovering. Small injuries began appearing. Hamstring tightness. Ankle inflammation. Fatigue late in matches. Her performance plateaued. Confidence dipped.

Nothing dramatic failed, she simply stopped improving. The eventual correction did not involve quitting NIL entirely. It involved reintroducing rest, reducing promotional frequency during season, and committing to one defined off-season window for physical rebuilding.

Within a year, development resumed. The problem was not visibility. It was an imbalance.

The College Perspective on Development

Any college strength coach can explain what separates high school athletes from college contributors, and the answer is rarely branding. It is almost always physical readiness and consistency.

College programs evaluate:

- Can this athlete handle structured lifting four days per week?
- Can they recover between travel and competition?
- Do they have movement discipline?
- Are they coachable under fatigue?

Those questions are answered through performance history, not "follower" counts. An athlete who uses high school to build physical durability enters college prepared, but an athlete who trades development time for visibility may enter college underprepared.

The distinction is rarely visible at age 16, but it becomes clear at age 19.

In-Season vs Off-Season Priorities

One of the simplest frameworks families can adopt is seasonal prioritization.

In Season

The primary focus for in-season should be performance, recovery, refinement and academic stability. NIL should be minimized and structured. Content can be batched, appearances limited, and filming consolidated.

Off Season

During the off-season, strength training, skill refinement, physical rebuilding and target exposure events can be introduced. NIL expansion is safer here, provided it does not interfere with training.

Scaling during season increases risk. Scaling during off-season allows breathing room. This is not about avoidance; it is about timing.

The Development Audit

At least twice per year, families should conduct a development audit. A development audit is when a family steps back and honestly evaluates where an athlete currently stands and what actually needs improvement before worrying about things like recruiting exposure or NIL opportunities.

Ask:

- Has performance measurably improved in the last 12 months?
- Has strength increased?
- Has speed improved?
- Has skill execution sharpened?
- Has endurance increased?
- Are injuries more frequent?
- Is sleep consistent?

If improvement has stalled while promotional commitments increased, reallocation may be necessary. Development is not accidental. It requires deliberate evaluation.

The Psychology of Early Recognition

It's a fact that recognition changes behavior. When a high school athlete is publicly affirmed through sponsorships, subtle identity shifts occur. They may feel pressure to "look the part."

They may prioritize aesthetic presentation over technical correction. They may resist feedback to protect public image.

Parents must guard against this drift.

Long-Term Athlete Development

Physical development in adolescence follows specific stages. These include growth spurts that alter coordination, gaining strength that follows neuromuscular adaptation, and additional power development following foundational strength.

These stages cannot be rushed through exposure. They are simply progressions in overall physical development. An athlete who commits to long-term progression often outperforms early standouts who plateau. NIL recognition at 15 does not guarantee dominance at 19. Trajectory matters more than timing.

When Development Creates Better NIL Later

Athletes who improve significantly during high school often become more marketable organically. Improvement leads naturally to higher competition levels, broader exposure, larger audiences, and increased credibility.

Disciplined sophomores who prioritize strength and skill may attract more substantial opportunities as a senior. Chasing early deals can cap that ceiling. But ironically, restraint early can increase leverage later.

What Parents Should Model

Parents set the tone. If parents speak primarily about deals, compensation, and exposure, athletes absorb that emphasis.

If parents speak primarily about effort, improvement, recovery, academics and how to be coachable, then their young athletes will internalize those values.

NIL should be discussed as responsibility, not reward.

The Quiet Competitive Advantage

Many athletes will pursue NIL aggressively. Some will overextend, others will burn out, and some will plateau under pressure. The athlete who quietly develops and who treats NIL proportionately while keeping training central, often gains competitive advantage without dramatic announcement.

High school careers are short but the physical foundation lasts.

A Tale of Two Weeks

Sometimes the difference between development and distraction is not dramatic. It is measured in hours.

Consider two hypothetical juniors in the same sport, at similar talent levels.

Athlete A — The Overextended Week

- 5 team practices
- 1 club session
- 1 lift

- 3 content filming sessions
- 2 brand planning calls
- Late-night editing twice
- Weekend appearance

Total added NIL time: 8–10 hours
Sleep averages 6.5–7 hours per night.

Recovery is inconsistent and performance is steady but not improving.

Athlete B — The "Development First" Week

- 5 team practices
- 2 structured lifts
- 1 mobility/recovery session
- 1 batched content session (90 minutes)
- No in-season appearances

Total added NIL time: 1.5–2 hours
Sleep averages 8+ hours.

Recovery is deliberate and performance trends upward.

The difference is allocation, not talent.

Small weekly imbalances accumulate over months. By senior year, those accumulated decisions widen performance gaps.

NIL does not need to disappear, but it does need to fit.

The Development Framework

Families often assume development "just happens" through team participation, but intentional development requires structure.
Here is a simple framework parents can implement without becoming overbearing:

1. Establish a Primary Focus Each Season

In-Season Focus:

- Tactical execution
- Game performance
- Maintenance strength

Off-Season Focus:

- Strength gain
- Speed improvement
- Technical correction
- Skill repetition

2. Track Measurable Metrics

Choose 3–5 measurable indicators relevant to the sport and test them quarterly:

- Vertical jump
- 40-yard dash time
- Mile time
- Exit velocity
- Shot percentage

- Serve speed
- Strength benchmarks

Improvement provides objective feedback.

3. Schedule Recovery

Recovery is not optional, build into the calendar:

- One full rest day per week
- Defined off-season break window
- Reduced load after tournament blocks
- If NIL commitments eliminate rest windows, adjust.

4. Reevaluate Every Six Months

Ask:

- Has performance improved?
- Has strength improved?
- Has speed improved?
- Has confidence improved?
- Has stress increased?

If the answer to improvement questions is "no," reassess allocation.

The Risk of Chasing Image Before Foundation

There is a natural desire to look ready before being ready. You may be tempted to invest in high-quality graphics and overlays for professional photos or an aggressive announcement schedule.

None of these replace foundational growth. In some cases, early overexposure increases pressure. Athletes begin to feel they must live up to an image instead of building quietly toward ability. As a result, their performance anxiety increases. Development thrives in environments where mistakes are allowed.

Being in the spotlight can complicate that.

When to Intentionally Say "Not Yet"

One of the most useful perspectives a parent can hold onto is the idea of "not yet." It creates space to slow things down when opportunities begin to expand. Instead of immediately taking on larger commitments, locking into longer-term agreements, or trying to scale activity during the season, families can choose to wait until the timing is right.

Holding back in those moments is not the same as missing out. In many cases, the athlete who takes time to develop physically and mentally is better prepared when bigger opportunities come along, and more capable of handling them in a way that supports both performance and long-term growth.

A Long-Term Example

Consider an athlete who prioritizes development from freshman through junior year.

- Minimal NIL exposure early.
- Structured training blocks.
- Consistent sleep.
- Stable academic performance.

By senior year, the progress is easier to see. Physical development, experience, and performance begin to show up consistently, and college interest often follows. As that happens, an athlete's audience tends to grow on its own, driven more by what they are doing in competition than by anything forced off the field.

When regional brands start to take interest, the situation looks different than it would have earlier. The athlete is in a stronger position to evaluate offers, manage their time, and handle added expectations. There is more confidence in decision-making, more structure in daily habits, and a better ability to deal with pressure as it comes.

Instead of chasing early validation, the athlete arrives at these opportunities with a sense of stability. Growth happens at a pace that matches their development, and the result is a more sustainable approach to NIL as those opportunities expand.

Development Is a Strategy

When others chase visibility, development becomes a strategic advantage. If half of athletes overextend themselves and half maintain disciplined development, separation occurs naturally over time.

High school sports reward durability, colleges reward projection.

Final Recalibration

Remember, NIL is not the enemy of development, but it can become one if boundaries dissolve. High school is not a marketing sprint. It is a developmental runway.

When families consistently ask: "Is this making my athlete better?"

rather than: "Is this increasing exposure?"

decisions clarify.

During this critical time, train first and build strength while sharpening skills and making sure academics don't slide. Also, don't overlook sleep, it can make a difference in all activities.

Then, if opportunities appear, integrate NIL proportionately.

A 12-Month Development Calendar Example

It can help to visualize how a development-first year actually unfolds. Imagine a high school sophomore in a spring sport.

January–February (Preseason Preparation)
Primary focus: strength building and skill refinement.

- 3 strength sessions per week
- Technical correction sessions
- Limited content creation (batched once per month)
- Sleep prioritized

March–May (In Season)
Primary focus: performance and recovery.

- 4-5 practices per week
- 1-2 maintenance lifts
- One defined NIL content session per week, capped at 90 minutes
- No additional appearances during heavy competition blocks

June–July (Off-Season Reset)
Primary focus: recovery and rebuilding.

- One full rest week
- Gradual reintroduction of strength training
- Optional, limited promotional work
- Skill-specific camps

August–October (Performance Growth Window)
Primary focus: measurable improvement.

- Structured speed training
- Position-specific refinement
- Evaluation testing
- NIL scaled only if time remains abundant

November–December (Academic & Recovery Emphasis
Primary focus: academic stability and light training.

- Recovery block
- Strategic planning for next year
- Review of performance metrics

This kind of rhythm prevents year-round fatigue.

If NIL commitments cannot fit cleanly inside that calendar without displacing training or recovery, something must give.

The Parent's Influence

Development-first culture does not happen accidentally; it happens when parents reinforce it consistently.

- When parents ask, "How did practice go?" before asking, "Did that post perform well?"
- When parents praise sleep discipline as much as sponsorship announcements.
- When parents say, "Let's review your lift numbers," before saying, "Let's check your followers."

These are small signals, but those small signals shape identity. If growth is emphasized, it becomes a priority.

The Long Game

High school NIL can feel urgent because visibility is immediate. Development is slower, but it compounds.

- A tenth of a second faster.
- Five pounds stronger.
- Ten percent more accurate.
- One year more mature.

Those marginal gains accumulate into meaningful separation by senior year. When athletes prioritize growth over exposure, they often find that exposure follows anyway.

Not because they chased it, but because they earned it.

A Final Perspective

There will always be athletes who accelerate early, just as there will always be headlines about young stars signing impressive deals. But most high school athletes are not competing in headlines. They are competing in gyms, fields, tracks, and pools, building capacity that no camera measures directly.

NIL can coexist with that process. But it cannot replace it.

If families keep development at the center, NIL becomes an accessory to growth rather than a distraction from it. And when opportunity grows later, whether in college or beyond, it will rest on something durable. Performance still wins because visibility without foundation rarely lasts.

What a Responsible High School NIL Deal Looks Like

FILM ROOM

The offer looked legitimate.

It came from a local coffee shop with a strong reputation in town, not to mention a family-owned business. They wanted a high school cross-country runner to post twice a month and appear at one Saturday community event.

The compensation: $500 per month and free merchandise.

Becky was excited but her parents were cautious. Nothing about the offer screamed "violation." It seemed clean since it wasn't tied to performance, connected to a booster club, or involved school logos.

But before saying yes, her family asked a different question:

- Not "Is this allowed?"
- Not "How much does it pay?"

They asked, "Does this look responsible?"

That is the lens this chapter is built around, because legality alone is not enough. Structure is.

The Anatomy of a Responsible NIL Deal

When it comes to lists, you either love them or hate them. Sometimes the most direct way of illustrating the characteristics of a responsible NIL deal is the best way. These include the following five characteristics:

- It is clearly tied to publicity value, not athletic performance.
- It is independent from school control or influence.
- It is proportionate in compensation.
- It is transparent.
- It is documented in writing.

If one of those pieces is missing, risk increases. If multiple elements are missing, pause.

Let's break those down carefully.

1. Compensation Must Be Tied to Publicity — Not Performance

A responsible deal pays the athlete for promotional activity such as:

- Social media posts
- Appearances
- Autograph sessions
- Product endorsements
- Commercial shoots
- Community events

It does not pay for:

- Points scored
- Playing time

- Wins
- Championships
- Remaining at a school
- Transferring to a school

A simple test helps: If the athlete is injured tomorrow and could not compete, would the deal still exist?

If the answer is yes, because the athlete still has visibility and audience, that's a good sign.

If the answer is no, because the payment depends on stats or participation — that's pay-for-play territory.

2. It Is Structurally Separate from the School

Responsible deals do not rely on:

- School logos
- School uniforms
- School facilities (unless properly rented like any public user)
- Coach coordination
- Booster funding tied to team interest

The deal should be between an athlete (and parents if they are a minor) and the business, not the school, coach or the booster club. Even casual involvement from a coach can blur perception. The more independent the structure, the cleaner the arrangement.

3. Compensation Is Proportionate

This is where maturity matters. If a local athlete with 1,200 followers is paid $10,000 for one post, administrators will ask questions. If that same athlete is paid $250 for two posts and a public appearance, this looks more aligned with local market value.

Proportionate does not mean small. It means reasonable relative to:

- Audience size
- Engagement rate
- Deliverables
- Local advertising norms

Responsible deals resemble marketing agreements, not inducements.

4. Transparency Exists Before and After

A responsible NIL deal is disclosed when required and is not hidden, secret, or outright say not to involve the school. When disclosure is required, submit it, keep all documentation, and definitely save email conversations.

Transparency reduces suspicion.

5. Get it Writing — Even If Simple

Verbal agreements create confusion. A responsible deal includes written terms covering:

- What is required
- When it is required
- How much will be paid
- When payment will be made
- Duration of agreement
- Termination rights

It does not need to be 20 pages, but it needs clarity.

FILM ROOM

Josh, a high school baseball player, was approached by a local training facility for a summer partnership. The initial verbal offer included:

- $1,000 per month
- Social posts
- Occasional lessons
- "Representing the program proudly"

That last phrase concerned his parents, so they asked for a written draft.

The written draft originally included language that stated: "Compensation is provided in recognition of athletic contributions to the community and continued participation in local softball programs."

That language was vague. Sure, it sounded harmless, but it could imply payment connected to participation, so they asked for revisions.

The final contract clarified: "Compensation is provided solely in exchange for promotional services described herein and is not contingent upon athletic performance, statistics, team membership, or enrollment decisions."

That sentence protected everyone, so the deal moved forward and no issues arose. That is what responsible structuring looks like.

Sample Responsible Contract Structure

Below is a simplified example of what a responsible high school NIL agreement might include.

Sample Structure (Educational Example Only)

Parties: [Business Name] and [Athlete Name]

Purpose: Athlete agrees to provide promotional services as described below.

Deliverables:

- Two Instagram posts per month.
- One in-person appearance (2 hours maximum).
- Tagging business account in relevant content.

Compensation: Business agrees to pay Athlete $400 per month for services rendered.

Payment Terms: Payment due within 10 days of deliverable completion.

No Performance Clause: Compensation is not contingent upon athletic performance, playing time, team membership, statistics, or enrollment decisions.

Independence Clause: This agreement is independent of any school or athletic association.

Duration: June 1 – August 31
Termination: Either party may terminate with written notice.

This structure does not eliminate all risk, but it does clarify intent.

Green Flags vs. Red Flags

Green Flags

- Clear deliverables.
- Reasonable compensation.
- Written agreement.
- Independent from school.
- Disclosure submitted when required.
- Payment schedule defined.
- No performance triggers.

Red Flags

- "We'll take care of you if you stay."
- Payment based on stats.
- Booster coordination.
- Pressure to keep quiet.
- Excessive compensation for minimal activity.
- School logo usage without permission.
- Contract language referencing team contribution.

Responsible NIL is actually boring. That is a compliment. If a deal feels dramatic, secretive, or urgent, go ahead and slow down.

What Most Responsible High School Deals Actually Look Like

Responsible deals are local, modest, and involve:

- Gyms
- Restaurants
- training facilities
- Apparel stores
- Community businesses
- Pay a few hundred dollars, sometimes a few thousand, over time

They rarely change a family's financial trajectory.

But they can teach business discipline, communication, contract awareness and also brand responsibility. This educational component is the hidden value.

Rare but Real: When Larger Deals Appear

Occasionally, a high-profile high school athlete may receive:

- Regional sponsorship
- Apparel partnerships
- National brand interest

In those rare cases, professional legal review becomes important and financial consultation becomes wise. Most readers of this book will not encounter this scenario, but if you do, scale your advisory team accordingly.

Structure must grow with exposure.

How to Evaluate an Offer Before Saying Yes

Before signing, ask:

- What exactly am I being paid to do?
- Is this tied in any way to performance or enrollment?
- Is compensation reasonable?
- Does this use school branding?
- Have we reviewed district policy?
- Is the agreement written clearly?
- Are termination terms fair?
- Is disclosure required?

If you cannot answer those confidently, pause. There is no penalty for asking for time to review.

There can be consequences for moving too quickly.

The Calm Warning

Most NIL problems do not start with bad intent. They start with:

- Assumptions
- Excitement
- Informal agreements
- Verbal promises
- Unclear language

Responsible deals feel slower and involve questions, edits, clarifications, and documentation. Remember, moving too quickly increases risk.

Breaking Down a Responsible Deal Frame by Frame

Let's slow this down and walk through one example carefully.

Scenario:
A junior track athlete with 3,800 Instagram followers and strong regional results is approached by a local physical therapy clinic.

The clinic proposes:

- $350 per month
- Two posts per month
- One seasonal appearance at a youth injury-prevention seminar
- Use of clinic apparel in training posts
- Six-month agreement

At first glance, this seems straightforward. But let's run it through the responsible deal lens.

Frame 1: What Is Being Purchased?

The clinic is purchasing visibility and credibility within the local athletic community. The deliverables are defined and measurable. Two posts. One appearance. That clarity is a positive signal. There is no language referencing race results, state qualification, or scholarship status. That matters.

Frame 2: Is Compensation Proportionate?

Local businesses often spend a few hundred dollars per month on digital ads. If this clinic would reasonably spend $300–$500 on targeted advertising, the compensation aligns with standard marketing budgets. This does not look like inducement-level money. It looks like a marketing expense, another positive signal.

Frame 3: School Separation

The agreement specifies that:

- No school logo may appear.
- No school facilities will be used.
- Promotional photos will be taken at a neutral training location.
- The athlete's school is not referenced in the contract, so the separation is clear.

Frame 4: Language Precision

The original draft included this line: "Compensation reflects the athlete's excellence in representing the local track community."

That language is vague. It could imply performance-based recognition.

The family requested a revision:

"Compensation reflects the athlete's agreement to provide promotional services as described."

This edit really matters. Responsible deals often hinge on small wording changes.

Frame 5: Disclosure

Before signing, the athlete's family emailed the athletic director: "We've been offered a small NIL agreement with a local clinic and want to confirm any district procedures we should follow."

The AD replied with a disclosure requirement and they complied. No surprise, no review, and more importantly no drama. The deal ran for six months without issue.

That is not flashy or viral, but it is stable.

When a Deal Looks Fine But Isn't

Sometimes the risk is not obvious.

Consider a basketball player offered $2,000 for a single post from a company owned by a major program booster. In addition, the post was published the week before a transfer window opened.

The contract says nothing about performance or about staying at the school. At least, nothing explicit. It looks like simple marketing. But in context, it certainly raises questions.

- Why the timing?
- Why the large amount?
- Why the connection to a booster with team influence?

Even if technically structured as NIL, perception may trigger review. High school athletics operate in communities where relationships matter. A responsible deal survives both contract and context review. If the surrounding circumstances create tension, that tension will eventually surface.

Understanding Market Value in High School NIL

Parents often ask, "What should my athlete charge?" That question is usually premature.

Market value in high school NIL is influenced by:

- Audience size
- Audience engagement
- Geographic location
- Sport visibility
- Deliverable quality
- Brand alignment

But here is the uncomfortable truth: Most high school athletes do not have national advertising value, even if they have community value. And when they do have that community value, it is usually modest. A local restaurant does not pay thousands for one post because it expects measurable return on investment. It pays modestly because it wants community connection.

When compensation exceeds logic, administrators notice. Responsible NIL rarely looks like a windfall. It looks like a fair exchange.

The Responsible Deal Stress Test

Before signing any agreement, run it through this structured filter.

- **Performance Independence Test**
  Would the deal exist if the athlete were temporarily injured?

- **School Separation Test**
  Does the agreement stand independently from school branding, personnel, and facilities?

- **Compensation Logic Test**
  Does the amount resemble a marketing budget or a recruitment incentive?

- **Disclosure Comfort Test**

  Would you be comfortable forwarding this contract to the athletic director?

- **Public Scrutiny Test**

  Would you feel comfortable if this agreement were printed in the local newspaper?

- **Longevity Test**

  Does this deal help the athlete grow — or does it over-commercialize them too early?

If the deal fails multiple tests, pause. Responsible NIL is rarely urgent.

FILM ROOM

Not every gray-area situation announces itself clearly.

Consider this example.

A senior quarterback is approached by a local car dealership for a seasonal endorsement. The dealership owner is also the largest annual donor to the football booster club. His name is on the scoreboard.

The offer includes:

- $4,000 for four posts
- One appearance at a promotional event
- The phrase "Proud to represent our championship program" in suggested caption language

On the surface, this is structured as NIL. There is no mention of performance bonuses or a written condition about staying at the school. But again, context matters.

First, the compensation amount is significantly higher than other local NIL deals in the community. Second, the dealership owner has deep involvement in the football program. Third, the caption language ties the endorsement to team identity. None of these factors alone create a violation. Together, they do increase scrutiny risk.

The responsible approach here would include:

- Removing team-representation language.
- Clarifying that compensation reflects promotional services only.
- Confirming disclosure with the athletic director.
- Evaluating whether the amount is proportionate to audience size.

Sometimes the responsible choice is not declining the deal but tightening its structure. The line between community support and inducement is not always bold. It is often contextual. Responsible families learn to see context, not just contract language.

Negotiation Is Allowed and Often Necessary

Many families assume NIL contracts are fixed. They are not.

If a business presents a draft agreement, you can:

- Request clarification.
- Adjust language.
- Ask for deliverable definitions.
- Modify duration.

- Clarify payment timing.
- Remove problematic phrases.

Negotiation does not signal hostility. It signals professionalism.

If a contract includes: "Compensation reflects the athlete's value to the team and community."

You can request: "Compensation reflects the athlete's promotional services as described."

That change may seem small. It meaningfully narrows interpretation. Similarly, if a contract does not specify payment timeline, ask for one.

"Payment due within 10 business days of deliverable completion" protects the athlete.

Responsible NIL includes teaching young athletes that contracts are discussions, not commands.

Exclusivity: A Clause That Deserves Attention

Some NIL agreements include exclusivity provisions.

For example: "Athlete agrees not to promote competing sports apparel brands during the term of this agreement."

In a professional setting, exclusivity is common. But at the high school level, exclusivity may be unnecessary or overly restrictive.

Before agreeing to exclusivity, consider:
- How long is the restriction?
- Does it limit future opportunities?

- Does it conflict with team-issued gear?
- Is compensation proportionate to the restriction?

An athlete who signs an exclusive deal with a small local apparel company may unintentionally limit future partnerships. Exclusivity should be weighed carefully, not accepted automatically.

Timing Matters

The timing of an NIL deal can change how it is viewed. Something that feels straightforward in July can raise questions by October, even if the terms have not changed. The difference is context.

During the season, the environment is more sensitive. Attention is already centered on competition, so any outside activity can take on added meaning. A deal introduced at that point may draw concerns about whether it is connected to performance, whether it could distract from the team, or whether it gains extra visibility because of what is happening on the field.

Outside the season, those same concerns tend to ease. There is more space to approach opportunities without the immediate connection to competition. Content can be created with more intention, and the separation from team activities is clearer. The structure of the deal may be identical, but the timing changes how it is perceived and evaluated.

This does not mean in-season deals are prohibited. It means they require heightened awareness. Families who intentionally structure NIL activity during off-season periods often encounter fewer complications.

The Long-Term Development Question

A responsible NIL deal should serve development, not distort it. For most high school athletes, development remains the priority. Strength training. Skill improvement. Academic progress. Team culture.

If NIL begins to dominate time, attention, or identity, recalibration may be necessary. NIL should supplement growth, not redirect it.

One More Micro Example

FILM ROOM

Erin, a sophomore swimmer with strong state-level results, is offered a modest partnership with a local nutrition store.

- The agreement includes:
- One post per month.
- Discounted supplements.
- A small quarterly payment.

Her parents hesitate because she is only a sophomore. In the end, they decide to proceed but limit the agreement to three months instead of a year.

Why?

Because development trajectory at that age is uncertain. Priorities may shift. Academic pressure may increase. A shorter contract allows flexibility. In other words, responsible structuring often means shorter initial commitments. Scaling can occur later if appropriate.

What This Chapter Really Comes Down To

At the high school level, most NIL opportunities will be small and will not change your family's finances, determine recruiting or define your athlete's future. What they can do is teach judgment. A responsible NIL deal is less about the amount of money involved and more about the habits it builds.

- Does your athlete read agreements carefully?
- Do they ask questions before signing?
- Do they understand what they are being paid to do?
- Do they separate their school identity from their personal brand?
- Do they think about perception as well as permission?

These habits matter far beyond high school sports.

When NIL is structured responsibly, it becomes a controlled environment to practice adulthood. When it is rushed or emotionally driven, it becomes noise.

Most high school athletes are still developing physically, academically, and socially. NIL should sit alongside that development, not distort it. If a deal feels stable, transparent, proportionate, and independent, it is probably aligned with the spirit of high school athletics. If it feels urgent, oversized, secretive, or emotionally charged, it deserves more time.

The most successful NIL paths at the high school level are not the most aggressive ones. They are the most deliberate, and deliberate decisions, repeated consistently, tend to compound in the right direction.

A responsible NIL deal does not need to be large. It needs to be clear. And at the high school level, growth is still the priority.

Financial Literacy for High School NIL: After the Check Arrives

FILM ROOM

When the first payment hit Ethan's account, it felt like validation.

It wasn't a massive deal. A local athletic apparel company paid him $3,000 over the course of the season for a handful of social media posts and two in-store appearances. For a high school junior, it felt significant and grown up.

His parents were supportive but pretty relaxed about the logistics. The payments came through electronically. When they did, Ethan used part of the money to buy new equipment and to upgrade his phone. He also treated teammates to dinner after a tournament win. The remainder sat in his account.

Then April arrived.

A thin envelope showed up in the mail, a Form 1099-NEC. His father had a vague memory of hearing that NIL income was "self-employment income," but it hadn't felt urgent when the money arrived. Now it was.

When they sat down with a tax preparer, the conversation changed quickly. Because Ethan had earned $3,000 in non-employee compensation, he owed self-employment tax, roughly 15.3%, plus federal income tax, and potentially state income tax depending on where they lived.

The number surprised them. After taxes, Ethan would keep significantly less than he had assumed. Nothing catastrophic happened, but the experience reframed the way they approached NIL income.

The lesson was not that NIL was a mistake. It was that income requires structure.

NIL Income Is Usually Self-Employment Income

Most high school NIL compensation is paid as independent contractor income.

That means:

- The athlete is not an employee.
- No taxes are withheld automatically.
- The athlete receives a 1099 form if earnings exceed $600 from a payer.
- The athlete is responsible for reporting and paying taxes.

This surprises many families. In traditional part-time employment, payroll taxes are withheld before a paycheck is issued. With NIL, the full amount often arrives untouched. It feels larger than it actually is. But the government still expects its share.

Example Math: What You Actually Keep

Let's walk through a simplified example.

Assume a high school athlete earns $5,000 in NIL income during the year.

Step 1: Self-Employment Tax

Self-employment tax covers Social Security and Medicare. It is approximately 15.3% of net earnings.
15.3% of $5,000 = $765.

Already, the usable amount drops to $4,235 before income tax.

Step 2: Federal Income Tax

Depending on total household income and filing structure, some of that $5,000 may fall into the 10% or 12% federal bracket.

Even conservatively, assume 10% on taxable income.
10% of $5,000 = $500.

Now we're down to roughly $3,735.

Step 3: State Income Tax (if applicable)

Some states impose income tax. If we estimate a modest 5% state tax:
5% of $5,000 = $250

That reduces usable income to approximately $3,485.

That $5,000 deal may realistically yield closer to $3,400–$3,700 after obligations.

This is not meant to discourage NIL participation. It is meant to recalibrate expectations.

Quarterly Payments: The Piece Families Overlook

If income becomes consistent or grows, families may need to consider quarterly estimated tax payments. The IRS expects self-employed individuals to make periodic payments if taxes owed exceed certain thresholds. Failing to do so can result in penalties.

This is where a CPA or tax professional becomes valuable.

Record Keeping Matters More Than You Think

Once income is involved, documentation becomes essential.

Athletes should maintain:

- Copies of all agreements
- Payment records
- Mileage logs (if travel is related to promotional activity)
- Receipts for legitimate business expenses
- Bank statements tied to NIL income

Without records, deductions are difficult to justify. With records, conversations become cleaner.

What Counts as a Deductible Expense?

High-level examples may include:

- Equipment purchased specifically for promotional activity
- Travel directly related to NIL appearances
- Marketing-related expenses

- Website hosting
- Professional photography for sponsored campaigns

However, not all training expenses automatically qualify. General athletic participation costs are often personal expenses, not business deductions. This is where professional guidance is important.

The goal is compliance, not aggressive interpretation.

The Separate Account Rule

One of the simplest protective steps a family can take is to create a separate bank account dedicated to NIL income. This separation creates clarity in income and expenses.

If NIL income is deposited into the same account used for groceries and daily expenses, tracking becomes messy.

A separate account allows:

- Clean income tracking
- Clear expense documentation
- Easier tax preparation
- Better financial awareness

For minors, this typically means a joint account with parental oversight. Transparency protects everyone involved.

Should a High School Athlete Form an LLC?

This question surfaces quickly. The short answer: usually not immediately.

An LLC can:

- Provide liability separation
- Add perceived professionalism
- Simplify certain tax considerations

But it also introduces:

- Filing requirements
- Annual fees (depending on state)
- Additional accounting complexity
- Administrative responsibility

For modest NIL income, say a few thousand dollars annually, an LLC may add more complexity than value. If income grows substantially or long-term brand development is occurring, revisit the conversation with a qualified professional.

You don't need to rush into it at this point.

The Roth IRA Conversation

One under-discussed benefit of earned income is retirement contribution eligibility. If a minor has earned income, they may qualify to contribute to a Roth IRA.

Why does this matter? These early contributions compound over time. Example:

If a 17-year-old contributes $3,000 to a Roth IRA and never adds another dollar, and that investment averages 7% annually, it could grow significantly over decades. The lesson is not to turn high school athletes into financial analyst; it is to recognize that even modest early income can create long-term benefit if handled thoughtfully.

Parents who treat NIL income as purely discretionary spending may miss an opportunity for education and long-term stability.

The 50/30/20 Framework (Adapted for NIL)

One simple model families can adapt:

- 50% reserved for taxes and savings
- 30% available for reinvestment into development
- 20% discretionary spending

This is not a rigid formula. Reserving half of incoming NIL income may feel conservative. But it creates margin.

Reinvesting Strategically

Reinvestment should not be impulsive.

Examples of thoughtful reinvestment:

- Strength and conditioning coaching
- Sport-specific training
- Academic tutoring
- Travel to high-level competitive events
- Professional editing for recruiting film
- Examples of impulsive spending:
- Excessive gear purchases
- Lifestyle upgrades unrelated to development
- Rapid equipment turnover without need

Money is a tool. Used intentionally, it supports growth.

Parental Oversight Without Overreach

Because most high school athletes are minors, parents remain financially and legally responsible in many respects.
That means:

- Contracts may require parental signature
- Tax filings often integrate into household filings
- Bank accounts are typically joint

Oversight is not distrust. The goal is not to control the athlete's money permanently. It is to teach responsible management gradually.

Financial literacy should increase as independence increases.

When Income Becomes Significant

When NIL income begins to reach a point where it meaningfully affects a family's finances, the situation changes. What may have started as a small, informal opportunity can begin to require more structure and oversight. At that stage, questions around how money is tracked, whether a formal business setup makes sense, how to handle potential liability, and how to plan financially all start to carry more weight.

This level of income is not common at the high school level, but it does happen on occasion. When it does, it is no longer something most families should try to manage on their own. Relying on general advice or piecing together information online can lead to mistakes. Professional guidance becomes an important part of handling that growth in a way that protects both the athlete and the family.

The Emotional Side of Money

Money sometimes changes things. Teammates may start to notice, other kids may talk, and expectations within the family can begin to shift.

That is where parents play an important role to keep things grounded and push back against any sense of entitlement that might develop. Earning NIL does not place an athlete above others on the team. If anything, it brings a higher level of responsibility.

High school locker rooms are often more sensitive than they appear. Small changes affect team dynamics. When financial success is handled with maturity and perspective, it helps protect those relationships.

A Better Outcome for Ethan

FILM ROOM

In Ethan's case, the tax surprise did not end his NIL participation, it refined it. The following year:

- A separate account was created.
- 50% of all NIL income was reserved immediately.
- A CPA consultation was scheduled.
- A portion was reinvested into offseason training.

The stress of April was replaced with predictability. The money did not disappear, but it became structured.

Calm Reality

Most high school NIL deals are modest and will not change a family's financial trajectory. But even modest income deserves disciplined handling.

NIL offers more than money. It offers a chance to teach budgeting, delayed gratification, taxes, long-term planning, and professional communication. All of these are valuable life skills both in and out of sports.

When Income Grows Faster Than Expected

Now consider a different scenario.

FILM ROOM

Emily, a senior basketball player, earns $18,000 over the course of a year through multiple small deals, apparel, a local restaurant, camp appearances, affiliate links. The money does not arrive in one lump sum. It arrives in fragments.

- $1,200 here.
- $750 there.
- $2,500 midseason.
- Affiliate commissions quarterly.

No single payment feels overwhelming, but cumulatively, the total is significant.

By year-end, she has not reserved funds consistently. Expenses were paid casually. Taxes were not calculated in real time. When tax preparation begins, the family learns that federal, state, and self-employment taxes may approach 25–35% depending on total household income. That can mean a liability of $5,000–$6,000.

If the money has already been spent, stress follows. Scaling income without scaling structure creates friction.

A Practical Quarterly Calendar

If NIL income becomes consistent, here is a simplified annual rhythm to follow.

January–March

- Track all income.
- Estimate projected total for the year.
- Consider first quarterly estimated tax payment if necessary.

April

- File prior year taxes.
- Review whether quarterly payments are needed.
- Adjust savings percentage if prior year was tight.

June

- Reassess income trajectory.
- Make second quarterly payment if required.

September

- Review cumulative income.
- Make third quarterly payment.

January (following year)

- Final estimated payment if necessary.

Not every athlete will need quarterly payments. But once income consistently exceeds several thousand dollars, it is worth discussing with a CPA. The goal is predictability, not panic.

What If No 1099 Arrives?

A common misconception is that if a company does not issue a 1099, the income does not need to be reported. This is incorrect. All earned income is reportable, regardless of whether or not a form is issued.

- Small local businesses sometimes fail to send paperwork.
- Digital platforms may pay through third-party processors.

The responsibility to report income still rests with the taxpayer. Record keeping protects you here.

Understanding "Net" vs "Gross"

Many athletes hear a deal amount and assume it represents usable money.

Example: A $10,000 NIL agreement may feel like a $10,000 benefit.

But if:

- 30% is reserved for taxes
- 20% is reinvested into training
- 10% is saved long term

Only 40% may be discretionary. That reframing changes how athletes evaluate opportunity.

Gross numbers impress. Net outcomes matter.

Deductions: Conservative Is Safer

There is a temptation to view every sports-related expense as deductible but be careful.

A few principles:

- The expense must be ordinary and necessary for the business activity.
- Personal expenses are generally not deductible.
- Training costs required for general athletic participation are often considered personal.

For example:

- If a photographer is hired specifically for a sponsored campaign, that may qualify as a business expense.
- If new cleats are purchased for regular team participation, that is typically personal.

Aggressive deduction strategies can create audit risk. Conservative reporting protects peace of mind.

Payment Schedules

Another overlooked element of financial literacy is payment timing.

Some deals pay:

- Upfront
- In installments
- After deliverables are completed
- Net-30 or net-60

Families should clarify:

- When payment will occur
- How it will be delivered
- What documentation accompanies it

Cash flow matters. An agreement promising $5,000 paid over ten months is different from $5,000 paid upfront. Budgeting must reflect this timing.

Teaching Spending Discipline

For many high school athletes, NIL income is their first meaningful money. In other words, spending discipline is not automatic.

Parents may consider:

- Requiring a written allocation plan before spending
- Encouraging a waiting period before major purchases
- Discussing long-term goals before discretionary use

Money earned quickly can be spent quickly. Money invested early compounds.

This is a great teaching moment. Handled thoughtfully, NIL income becomes a financial literacy course more effective than any classroom lecture.

Guarding Against Financial Exploitation

Although it is not common at the high school level, the risk of financial exploitation is real. As an athlete gains visibility, the attention they receive is not always limited to legitimate opportunities. Situations can arise where there is pressure to put money into unfamiliar ventures, requests for loans from friends or extended family, or offers from adults who present "investment opportunities" without clear details. In some cases, contracts may be structured in ways that quietly shift an unfair share of earnings away from the athlete.

These situations often develop gradually, which is why parental oversight matters. As recognition grows, so does the likelihood of encountering people or proposals that go beyond standard endorsements. When something feels rushed, unclear, or unnecessarily complicated, it is usually a sign to slow down and take a closer look.

Seeking professional guidance at that point is a practical step, not an overreaction. The cost of getting clear advice is typically far less than the potential impact of making a decision without it.

When to Involve a Professional

Consider consulting a CPA or financial professional when:

- Income exceeds $10,000–$15,000 annually
- Multiple income sources exist
- Quarterly payments may be required
- An LLC or business structure is being considered
- Multi-year agreements are signed

Professional guidance does not mean loss of control.

A Conversation Framework for Families

At the beginning of each NIL year, consider sitting down together and discussing:

- What is our projected income?

- What percentage will be reserved for taxes?
- What percentage will be saved?
- What percentage will be reinvested?
- What are long-term goals?
- What documentation system will we use?

Writing these decisions down reduces confusion later.

The Psychological Reset

Money introduces a variety of emotions including excitement, validation, pressure, and expectations. An intentional system neutralizes the emotional considerations. This can include automatic transfers to savings, reserving funds for taxes and structured reinvestment.

An athlete who sees half of each deposit moved immediately into reserved categories begins to understand financial reality quickly. That understanding is empowering.

Financial Maturity Is a Competitive Advantage

College programs increasingly value maturity. An athlete who understands:

- Contracts
- Taxes
- Documentation
- Professional communication

enters higher levels with confidence.

An athlete who treats money casually often struggles when stakes increase. Financial literacy may not improve jump height or pitch velocity, but it improves stability.

The Higher Earner

While rare at the high school level, some athletes will earn amounts that materially affect family finances. Consider a senior swimmer who qualifies for national-level competition and signs multiple sponsorships. Over 12 months, she earns $28,000.

That number changes conversations.

Now:

- Quarterly estimated payments are likely required.
- Self-employment tax alone may exceed $4,000.
- Federal and state income tax could push total obligations above $8,000 depending on household income.
- Savings decisions become more strategic.
- College financial aid implications may need review.

At this level, informal tracking is no longer sufficient. Professional accounting becomes a reasonable investment.

The key distinction is this: most high school athletes will never approach this level of income.

But if income accelerates unexpectedly, structure must accelerate with it. Scaling income without scaling systems creates instability, but scaling both together preserves calm.

A Practical Allocation Worksheet

Parents often ask, "How much should we set aside?" There is no universal percentage. But here is a conservative framework you can adapt.

When NIL income is received:

Step 1 — Immediately reserve 30–35% for taxes.

If income grows, increase that percentage.

Step 2 — Allocate 20–30% to long-term savings.

Options may include:

- High-yield savings
- Roth IRA (if eligible)
- College expenses
- Long-term investment vehicle

Step 3 — Allocate 20–30% for reinvestment.

Examples:

- Strength coaching
- Sport-specific training
- Academic tutoring
- Recruiting film production
- Travel to legitimate competitive events

Step 4 — Limit discretionary spending to 10–20%.

This preserves enjoyment without destabilizing the system. When athletes see that most of their income is allocated strategically, they begin to understand that earnings are a tool, not a lifestyle.

The Aid and Eligibility Conversation

Another rarely discussed element is how income may affect:

- Need-based financial aid
- FAFSA calculations
- Household income reporting

While modest income often has limited impact, higher earnings can shift aid formulas. Families with significant NIL income should consult a financial aid advisor before assuming eligibility will remain unchanged. This is not a reason to avoid NIL. It is a reason to understand full context.

The Social Pressure Factor

Money changes peer dynamics. Teammates may assume income equals wealth. In turn, friends may expect generosity. Extended family members may view the athlete differently.

Attitudes change. It is important to prepare athletes for this. Clear messaging helps: "This income is structured. A large portion is reserved. It is not free spending money."

Financial maturity sometimes requires quiet boundaries. Saying no to lending requests or impulsive spending is part of growth. Parents should normalize that restraint.

Identity Before Income

At the high school level especially, income must never become an identity. An athlete is not more valuable or mature because they sign deals. They are also not more established because their name appears on a banner.

Money is temporary but character compounds.

If NIL income disappears tomorrow, the athlete's development, habits, and discipline remain. That is why this chapter matters. The goal is not to maximize income. It is to maximize maturity.

A Different Ending for Ethan

Let's return briefly to Ethan.

FILM ROOM

The first year caught his family off guard. Taxes felt frustrating. The paperwork felt adult and inconvenient. But the second year looked different.

When his first payment arrived, half of it was moved immediately into a separate savings bucket. A portion went into a Roth IRA. Another portion was reserved for offseason training with a strength coach. He still spent some of it. He bought new cleats. He took his younger sister out for dinner. He felt the reward for his effort.

But something subtle shifted.

He began asking different questions:

- "How much should I set aside for taxes on this one?"
- "Is this deal worth the time it's taking?"
- "If I reinvest this, does it make me better?"

The money educated him.

By senior year, when a larger regional sponsorship arrived, he was calm. He read the contract carefully. He tracked deliverables. He understood net income versus gross. The opportunity did not overwhelm him because the habits were already in place.

This is the real value of handling NIL income responsibly.

Money as a Mirror

Money amplifies who an athlete already is. If they are disciplined, money reinforces discipline. If they are impulsive, money magnifies impulsiveness.

This is why parental modeling matters so much. When parents respond to NIL income calmly — not emotionally — athletes follow that lead. When parents prioritize long-term stability over short-term excitement, athletes internalize that hierarchy.

Financial literacy is not about spreadsheets. It is about character under responsibility.

The Real Win

Most high school NIL income will never be life-changing.

But if the athlete:

- Tracks income
- Reserves taxes
- Saves intentionally
- Reinvests strategically
- Avoids pressure
- Asks professionals when needed

Then those skills are life-changing and extend far beyond athletics. Whether an athlete continues into college sports, professional sport, business, or an entirely different field, disciplined financial habits compound quietly.

Closing Perspective

If handled carelessly, NIL income creates stress. If handled strategically, it becomes:

- A budgeting lesson
- A tax education
- A savings foundation
- A professional communication exercise
- A maturity accelerator

High school is not the time to build a lifestyle around endorsement income. It is the time to build financial habits that will endure far beyond it. Most NIL money earned in high school will be modest. But the habits built during that time can influence decades.

When the check arrives, pause and reserve future funds first, plan for the rest, and spend last. This order rarely fails.

Contracts, Agents, Representation, and Professionals

FILM ROOM

The message arrived on a Tuesday night.

"Hey, saw your highlights. I represent multiple athletes in your region and think we could build your NIL profile quickly. Let's talk."

For Jake, a junior wide receiver with growing visibility, it felt validating. The message came from someone who listed himself as a "sports marketing consultant." His bio included several college athletes and a few professional names.

The family had not been looking for representation. They had signed two modest local NIL deals on their own. Nothing complicated. But the message introduced a new question: Are we supposed to have an agent?

It's a common moment, and it deserves a calm answer.

What Agents Actually Do

At a high level, sports agents typically:

- Negotiate contracts
- Identify sponsorship opportunities
- Coordinate brand partnerships
- Manage endorsement logistics
- Advise on public positioning
- Take a percentage of compensation

That sounds attractive, but there's a critical distinction: Those services are most valuable when income is complex, multi-layered, or substantial.

At the high school level, most NIL deals are:

- Local
- Modest
- Short-term
- Straightforward

Negotiating a $1,200 equipment sponsorship rarely requires formal representation. More so, coordinating two social media posts and a local appearance does not demand a professional intermediary. Representation adds value when complexity increases. Until then, it may add cost without adding leverage.

Most High School Athletes Do Not Need Immediate Representation

When I say this, don't think I am anti-agent. I previously worked in Hollywood, so I know how valuable agents and managers can be and how they can help guide a career. But there are some things we really need to remember here.

If an athlete:

- Has signed one or two local deals
- Earns under $10,000 annually
- Has simple deliverables
- Is not fielding multi-brand negotiations

formal representation may not be necessary, even if they come knocking on your door or sliding into your athlete's DMs. Parents often underestimate their ability to handle modest agreements with basic diligence.

- Reading contracts.
- Clarifying payment terms.
- Ensuring compliance.
- Communicating professionally.

These are manageable skills. If you are using this book and applying its guidance carefully, you are already ahead of many families. Having representation is not a prerequisite for legitimacy.

Understanding Common Commission Structures

Agents are typically compensated via a commission. Common ranges include:

- 10–20% of NIL compensation
- Sometimes higher for smaller deals
- Sometimes tiered based on deal size

Here's an example:

- If an athlete signs a $5,000 deal and the commission is 20%, the agent receives $1,000.
- If the agent negotiated a materially better agreement, say increasing the deal from $3,000 to $5,000, that commission may feel justified.
- If the agent simply facilitated a deal the family could have executed independently, the value calculation changes.

Commission percentages should be clearly stated in writing. Flat monthly retainers at the high school level should be approached cautiously. Choosing representation should align with revenue, not precede it.

Athlete-Agent Laws (Conceptually)

Most states have laws regulating athlete agents. These laws often require:

- Registration
- Disclosure
- Written contracts
- Specific cancellation rights

The purpose of these regulations is consumer protection.

Families should confirm that any individual representing themselves as an agent is:

- Properly registered if required in the state
- Willing to provide documentation
- Transparent about compensation structure

If someone avoids documentation, downplays paperwork, or resists disclosure, pause. Legitimate professionals welcome clarity and will gladly provide their documentation and licenses.

"Advisors" and Informal Representatives

Some individuals avoid the term "agent" and instead describe themselves as:

- Marketing advisors
- Brand consultants
- Talent managers
- NIL strategists

These titles can vary. The function matters more than the label. If the person is:

- Negotiating contracts
- Receiving commissions
- Representing the athlete in financial matters

they are functioning as a representative, whether they use the title or not. In these cases, compensation terms should still be documented. Transparency is non-negotiable.

Social Media Managers: Pros and Cons

Another growing area is outsourced social media management.

Pros:

- Professional content quality
- Posting consistency

- Strategic branding
- Time savings

Cons:

- Monthly cost
- Potential loss of authentic voice
- Reduced personal oversight
- Risk of tone misalignment

For most high school athletes, authenticity matters more than polish. A slightly imperfect but genuine voice often resonates better than curated branding. It is usually easy to tell whether an athlete is posting personally or someone else is managing the account.

If outsourcing social media is considered, ask:

- Does this free meaningful development time?
- Is the cost proportional to income?
- Is the athlete comfortable with reduced control?
- Outsourcing should simplify life, not complicate it.

Parents as Managers

In many high school cases, parents function as de facto managers. I saw this in Hollywood as well with mixed results. Sometimes things go awry. But let's examine some of the strengths and risks with having a parent act as a manager for their child.

Strengths:

- Deep trust
- Alignment of priorities
- No commission cost

- Direct oversight

Risks:

- Emotional negotiation
- Time burden
- Strained parent–child dynamics
- Overextension

Parents who manage deals must separate emotional advocacy from business negotiation. That can be difficult. Keeping communication professional protects both relationships and outcomes. If a parent feels overwhelmed or conflicted, it may be time to seek limited professional review, not necessarily full representation.

When parents act as managers, emotional neutrality becomes critical.

Questions parents must ask themselves:

- Am I negotiating based on pride?
- Am I overvaluing small deals?
- Am I letting my child's recognition influence my judgment?

One advantage parents hold is long-term perspective. They are less likely to push for short-term exposure at the expense of development. But they must guard against becoming overprotective gatekeepers who stifle growth.

When Representation Actually Makes Sense

Representation becomes reasonable when:

- Income exceeds $15,000–$20,000 annually
- Multiple brands are negotiating simultaneously
- Contract language becomes complex
- Long-term agreements are involved
- National exposure increases

Time demands interfere with school or training

In those cases, professional negotiation may add measurable value. The key is that representation follows traction, it should not be the first step.

Red Flags

Balanced but firm means naming warning signs clearly.

Be cautious if someone:

- Promises guaranteed deals
- Requests fees upfront without performance alignment
- Pressures quick signatures
- Discourages parental involvement
- Refuses written agreements
- Cannot clearly explain compensation structure
- Inflates projected earnings unrealistically

High school athletes are not professional free agents. Anyone who treats them that way prematurely may not be aligned with long-term development.

An Evaluation Checklist

If considering representation, some questions you should ask are:

- What specific value are you adding?
- How are you compensated?
- Is your commission tied only to deals you secure?
- Are you registered if required by state law?
- How long is the agreement term?
- What is the termination clause?
- Are there exclusivity provisions?
- Can we consult independent legal review?

Professional representatives answer these calmly and don't deflect answers or talk in circles. Defensiveness is a signal to walk away.

The Parent–Agent Interview Script

If you meet with a potential representative, consider asking:

- What high school athletes do you currently represent?
- What was their average annual NIL income before and after working with you?
- How do you source opportunities?
- What is your commission structure?
- Are you registered under applicable state athlete-agent laws?
- How long is your agreement term?
- Can we review a sample agreement?
- How do you handle conflict of interest?

- Do you carry professional liability insurance?
- How do you separate high school from collegiate clients?

Clear, confident answers signal professionalism.

Legal Review vs Full Representation

Sometimes a family does not need an agent, but they might need a lawyer to review a contract. This can be a one-time occurrence or may happen several times when deals are proposed. Paying a flat fee for contract review may be more appropriate than entering a commission-based relationship.

This preserves control while ensuring protection. Complexity should determine support level.

Empowering Perspective

The presence of representation does not determine legitimacy. Some of the most stable high school NIL experiences involve:

- Modest deals
- Direct communication
- Parental oversight
- Clear documentation
- Conservative scaling

Representation is a tool and tools are useful when needed, but unnecessary tools add weight. If an athlete's NIL activity is small, structured, and manageable, you are not behind because you lack an agent, you are proportional.

If activity grows beyond your comfort or expertise, bringing in professional support becomes a strategic decision, not a reactive one.

When Early Representation Goes Wrong

FILM ROOM

Louisa is a sophomore basketball player who begins to gain regional attention. After one breakout tournament, two different individuals reach out to her offering representation.

One promises brand deals within weeks; another suggests building a "national NIL strategy." The family, feeling unprepared and flattered, signs a one-year exclusive agreement with a 20% commission.

Within six months:

- No new deals materialize.
- The agent occasionally forwards generic marketing emails.
- A local business approaches the athlete directly, but the agent insists on negotiating and requests commission on the deal.
- Communication becomes sporadic.

The family begins to feel stuck because the agreement includes exclusivity and a long-term, exiting is not simple. Now, 20% of everything must pass through a third party.

The issue here was not dishonesty, it was misalignment. Louisa's representation preceded traction. In other words, the tool came before the need.

What a Representation Agreement Typically Includes

Before signing any representation agreement, families should understand its components.

Common sections include:

Term Length

How long does the agreement last?

- 6 months?
- 1 year?
- Multiple years?

Shorter initial terms are generally safer. Long multi-year agreements for high school athletes deserve careful review.

Exclusivity

Is the agent the exclusive representative for:

- All NIL deals?
- Only certain categories?
- Only specific geographic areas?

Having exclusivity limits flexibility. If exclusivity is broad, the athlete may be unable to negotiate independently.

Commission Structure

Commission may be:

- A flat percentage of all compensation
- A percentage only on deals secured by the agent
- Tiered based on deal size

Families should clarify whether the agent earns commission on deals the athlete independently sources. That distinction matters.

Payment Timing

- When does the agent receive commission?
- Upon signing a contract?
- Upon athlete receiving payment?
- Upon invoice completion?

Commission should align with actual payment received.

Termination Clause

How can the agreement be ended?

- For cause?
- With notice?
- Immediately?
- With financial penalty?

High school athletes benefit from agreements that include clear exit mechanisms.

Post-Term Commission

Some agreements include clauses allowing the agent to receive commission on deals signed after termination if they were "in progress" during representation.

This language should be read carefully, since vague definitions create confusion.

A Case Where Representation Adds Value

Now consider a different scenario.

FILM ROOM

Sarah, a senior gymnast, qualifies for national competition. Multiple brands reach out to her simultaneously.

The offers vary significantly in:

- Compensation
- Deliverables
- Usage rights
- Duration

One agreement includes a broad image usage clause that would allow the brand to use the athlete's likeness indefinitely.

With all these offers coming in at the same time, each with different requirements, the family feels out of depth. They consult a licensed sports marketing attorney for contract review and, eventually, sign with a representative specializing in Olympic-level NIL.

The representative:

- Narrows usage rights
- Increases compensation
- Shortens contract duration
- Aligns payment schedule with competition calendar

In this case, professional expertise created measurable improvement. Representation followed complexity. That's the pattern you want.

The Social Media Manager Dilemma

FILM ROOM

Paula, a junior volleyball player, has decided to hire a social media consultant charging $1,000 per month.

The consultant promises:

- Content strategy
- Daily posting
- Brand alignment
- Audience growth

Within three months:

- Posting frequency increases.
- Visual polish improves.
- Follower count rises modestly.

But:

- Paula spends more time filming.
- Captions no longer sound authentic.
- School coaches notice increased distraction.
- Income remains flat.

The cost exceeds the return.

Contrast that with a different athlete who:

- Batches content once weekly.
- Uses a freelance editor for specific campaigns.
- Maintains personal voice.
- Keeps expenses proportional.

Outsourcing is not wrong, but it should be driven by:

- Revenue
- Time efficiency
- Strategic need

Not ego.

The Psychology of Early Validation

Having representation or having someone approach you offering to represent your athlete, can feel like arrival and signal importance. But high school athletes must resist the idea that signing an agent equals advancement.

Representation is not status, it is logistics. If logistics are simple, representation may be premature.

Families should ask: Does this arrangement increase our control, or decrease it? If communication slows, transparency reduces, and decision-making shifts away from the athlete and family, reassess. Professional help should expand clarity, not replace it.

When to Revisit the Conversation

If you have been approached and decided against representation, that doesn't mean the subject will never come up again. Revisit representation when:

- Income consistently exceeds $20,000 annually.
- National brands are negotiating.
- Contract language becomes complex.
- Time demands interfere with development.
- Legal exposure increases.

At that point, representation may feel like relief rather than pressure.

The Empowering Close

Jake's family did something simple: they paused. They did not reject representation permanently.

Instead, they asked: "Do we need this right now?" The honest answer was no.

For now, they continued building locally.

- They learned about contracts.

- They managed finances.
- They protected development.

Two years later, when national interest increased, they entered conversations confidently — not desperately.

That is empowerment.

You do not need to rush into representation to be legitimate, you need to understand when it serves you. Professional help is a tool. At the high school level, clarity is often more valuable than delegation.

A Clause-by-Clause Example

Below is a simplified example of language families may encounter in a representation agreement. This is not legal advice, but it illustrates what to watch for.

Exclusivity Clause Example:

"Athlete hereby appoints Representative as the exclusive marketing agent for all Name, Image, and Likeness activities during the Term."

Commentary:

This language is broad. It means the representative earns commission on every NIL deal, even those independently secured by the athlete.

Families should ask:

- Can exclusivity be limited to deals the agent sources?
- Can exclusivity be limited to certain categories?
- Can the athlete retain the right to independently negotiate local deals?

Broad exclusivity without performance benchmarks is risky at the high school level.

Commission Clause Example:

"Representative shall receive 20% of all gross compensation earned by Athlete during the Term."

Commentary:

"Gross compensation" means before taxes, expenses, or deductions. Families should clarify:

- Is commission calculated on gross or net?
- Are reimbursed expenses included?
- Are bonuses included?

Small wording differences affect real money.

Term Clause Example:

"This Agreement shall remain in effect for twenty-four (24) months."

Commentary:

Two years is significant in high school athletics. If performance stalls, priorities shift, or development needs change, exiting a long agreement becomes complicated.

Shorter initial terms (6–12 months) provide flexibility.

A Commission Conflict Scenario

Imagine a high school senior signing with a representative at 20% commission.

A local restaurant, owned by a longtime family acquaintance, approaches the athlete directly for a $4,000 promotional agreement. The family negotiates independently, but the representative insists on collecting 20% commission because the agreement was signed during the representation term. $800.

The family feels frustrated. The representative argues the contract language supports their claim.

This conflict was entirely avoidable. If the agreement had specified commission only on deals secured by the representative, clarity would have existed from the beginning.

Commission structures must match actual value delivered.

The "Family Friend Advisor" Risk

Another situation that comes up fairly often involves a well-meaning family friend offering to step in and "help manage things." The intent is usually positive. They may have business experience, local connections, or simply want to support the athlete's success. At first, it can feel like a natural and low-risk way to handle new opportunities.

Problems surface when that help is not clearly defined. Without structure, simple questions can turn into points of confusion. It may not be clear what their role actually includes. If nothing is written down, assumptions can take the place of agreement, and expectations can drift over time.

When money becomes part of the relationship, even small misunderstandings can create tension. What started as support can strain the relationship if roles and compensation are not clearly established from the beginning. Taking the time to document expectations and define responsibilities protects both the athlete and the person trying to help.

Exclusivity

Exclusivity deserves deeper examination. At the professional level, exclusivity is standard in contracts and agreements. At the high school level, exclusivity can be premature.

If an athlete signs an exclusive agreement:

- All negotiations flow through one person.
- All brand contact is filtered.
- Flexibility decreases.

If the representative is highly active and skilled, this may work. If activity slows or communication lags, the athlete's momentum slows as well.

Families should consider:

- Including performance benchmarks
- Allowing partial exclusivity
- Negotiating shorter terms
- Building in early termination clauses

Representation should accelerate opportunity, not gatekeep it.

Performance Benchmarks in Agreements

Few high school families think to negotiate performance benchmarks. Examples might include:

- Minimum number of outreach attempts per quarter
- Minimum number of brand proposals submitted
- Quarterly performance reviews

If a representative expects commission, families can reasonably expect measurable effort. Professional relationships are reciprocal.

The Emotional Component of Signing

Signing with representation feels like progress and can feel like validation. But families must separate emotion from evaluation.

Ask:

- Are we signing because we feel pressure?
- Are we signing because income justifies it?
- Are we signing because we fear missing out?
- Are we signing because this representative has a clear, defined role?
- Are we signing because we understand exactly how they are compensated?
- Are we signing because this improves the athlete's current situation, not just future possibilities

Fear-based decisions rarely age well, but clarity-based decisions do.

A Positive Representation Example

FILM ROOM

Connor, a senior track athlete, begins receiving interest from national brands before graduation. His schedule becomes suddenly crowded with:

- Negotiation emails
- Contract revisions
- Usage rights questions
- Appearance logistics
- Payment coordination

His training time begins to shrink.

In this case, hiring a professional representative allows:

- Centralized negotiation
- Contract review
- Brand coordination
- Time protection

Performance improves because distraction decreases. This is appropriate delegation.

Representation worked because it solved a real bottleneck.

Control vs. Convenience

The real question families must ask is: Are we giving up control for convenience?

If convenience solves complexity, that may be wise. But if convenience simply replaces manageable effort, it may not be necessary.

High school NIL does not require infrastructure at the outset.

The Empowered Position

It is easy to feel like you are falling behind without representation, but that is not the reality. Families who handle smaller, local opportunities on their own are not being unprofessional, and choosing to grow at a steady pace does not mean missing out. In many cases, it reflects a more controlled and thoughtful approach.

Representation is not a milestone to reach for its own sake. It is a business decision, and like any business decision, it should be tied to real needs such as increasing revenue, added complexity, or limited time. When those factors are not present, bringing in outside help too early can create more complications than benefits.

Over time, as experience builds, the picture becomes clearer. There comes a point when additional support genuinely adds value, and that moment is usually easy to recognize. By then, there is a stronger understanding of how contracts work, how commissions are structured, how agreements are organized, and where real leverage exists. That foundation allows decisions to be made with confidence instead of urgency.

A Final Perspective on Representation

Representation at the high school level is not inherently good or bad, it is situational. Some athletes will reach a point where professional negotiation meaningfully increases opportunity, protects time, and improves contract terms. In those cases, representation is a tool used wisely.

Others will never need formal representation during high school. Their NIL activity will remain local, manageable, and modest. For them, clear communication, parental oversight, and disciplined structure are more than sufficient.

The mistake is not hiring an agent too late, the mistake is hiring one too early before complexity justifies it, before leverage exists, before systems are in place.

Representation should:

- Solve problems
- Reduce strain.
- Increase clarity.

If it creates confusion, pressure, or loss of control, something is misaligned. Parents sometimes worry that declining representation signals inexperience. In reality, thoughtful timing signals maturity.

Remember:

- You are allowed to ask questions.
- You are allowed to request revisions.
- You are allowed to seek independent legal review.
- You are allowed to say no.

Professional relationships are partnerships, not favors.

The most empowered families approach representation calmly. They do not rush. They do not sign out of flattery. They evaluate value, structure, and fit. If NIL activity grows to the point where representation becomes helpful, you will recognize it because it will feel like relief, not urgency. Until then, clarity, documentation, and proportional growth will carry you further than delegation ever could.

Chapter 12: Recruiting Myths Parents Still Believe

Part I — The Pressure Machine

FILM ROOM

The email arrived at 10:42 p.m., about twenty minutes after the highlight video went live.

"Your son has been identified as a prospect with collegiate potential. For a limited time, we can build his recruiting profile and distribute it to over 300 college programs."

- It referenced exposure.
- It referenced access.
- It referenced urgency.
- The price was $1,495.

Caleb's father had just finished watching the film again. The game had been one of Caleb's best performances all season. He looked bigger. Faster. More confident. Teammates were tagging him online. A few parents had mentioned "next level potential" in the stands. Momentum feels powerful and fragile in youth sports.

- What if this is the moment?
- What if we miss it?
- What if everyone else is already doing this?

Recruiting culture thrives in that emotional window, right after the performance high, right before clarity returns.

The email was not necessarily a scam. The company had testimonials and a website. It had a clean logo and a video explaining its services. But what it also had, and what most recruiting marketing leverages, was urgency.

- "Limited time."
- "Selected prospect."
- "Immediate distribution."
- "Big audience."

Caleb's father did something that many families struggle to do in that moment: he waited. He closed the laptop. He went to bed. He revisited the email the next morning. And when the emotion settled, the questions changed. Instead of asking, "What if we fall behind?" he asked, "What are we actually buying?"

That shift, from fear to evaluation, is the foundation of this chapter. Recruiting is real. Opportunity does exist. Scholarships are earned every year by disciplined athletes. But the ecosystem around recruiting is loud. And when it's loud, myths travel faster than facts.

Before we talk about timelines, scholarships, or NIL visibility, we need to address the machine itself. Recruiting has become an industry and where there is industry, there is marketing. Where there is marketing, there is exaggeration. And where there is exaggeration, there are myths.

Myth #1: NIL Gets You Recruited

At this point in the book, you understand what NIL actually is: the ability to monetize publicity rights. But somewhere in youth sports culture, a quiet assumption has taken hold: that visibility equals recruitment.

Let's separate two realities.

- College coaches recruit athletes to fill roster needs.
- Brands partner with athletes to leverage audience engagement.

Those are different evaluation systems.

A high school athlete with a local gym sponsorship may demonstrate initiative and community engagement. That's certainly positive.

But a college coach is still asking:

- Can this athlete help us compete?
- How does this athlete project physically at our level?
- Does this athlete fit our positional scheme?
- Does this athlete align academically?

NIL presence does not override skill gaps.

In some cases, heavy branding without corresponding performance can create quiet skepticism. Coaches may wonder whether the athlete's focus is split. That does not mean NIL is harmful, it means it is supplemental.

For most high school athletes, recruiting success creates NIL opportunity later, not the reverse. The arrow points from performance to visibility, not visibility to performance.

Understanding that direction reduces unnecessary pressure.

Myth #2: If We Don't Start Early, We'll Fall Behind

The acceleration of youth sports has been dramatic.

- Middle school athletes attend national showcases.
- Freshmen build recruiting profiles.
- Parents track rankings before driver's licenses.

Early development is valuable. Early marketing is often premature. In most sports, meaningful recruiting evaluation begins:

- Sophomore year at the earliest
- Junior year more commonly
- Senior year for many late developers

Yes, there are exceptions, particularly in certain high-visibility sports. But even in those cases, physical maturity and projection still drive decisions. A third grader does not need an NIL strategy. A seventh grader does not need a national recruiting platform.

They need:

- Development
- Skill acquisition
- Strength progression
- Game understanding
- Emotional maturity

Recruiting rewards readiness at the right time, it does not reward premature exposure.

The fear of being "behind" often originates from social comparison — not from actual recruiting data.

Myth #3: Exposure Equals Opportunity

Exposure feels proactive. It feels like motion. It feels like doing something. But exposure without readiness produces silence.

College coaches operate within time constraints. They review hundreds, sometimes thousands, of prospects. When they view film, they are making rapid evaluations. If an athlete is not physically ready, technically polished, or positionally competitive, the coach moves on.

Rarely will a coach revisit a sophomore two years later unless the athlete re-initiates contact with significantly improved film. Timing matters. Being seen too early can close mental tabs. That is why development-first strategy is not passive. It is strategic timing.

You want exposure when performance peaks, not before it matures.

A Recruiting Timeline by Grade

Let's slow this down and build a realistic developmental arc.

Elementary School

Focus: Fun, fundamentals, multi-sport development.
NIL relevance: Essentially none.
Recruiting relevance: None.

The goal is love of sport and foundational movement.

Middle School

Focus: Skill refinement, competitive growth, physical development.
Recruiting relevance: Minimal. Some athletes may begin attending camps, but recruiting communication is rarely meaningful at this stage.
NIL relevance: Rare and typically unnecessary.

The focus remains development.

Freshman Year

Focus: Adjustment to varsity pace (if applicable), strength development, academic stability.
Recruiting relevance: Limited. Coaches may begin tracking prospects in some sports, but evaluation remains preliminary.
NIL relevance: Local and modest at best.

This is not the stage for aggressive marketing.

Sophomore Year

Focus: Physical growth, performance consistency.
Recruiting relevance: Increasing. Film begins to matter more. Direct communication may begin in certain sports.
NIL relevance: Still secondary.

If NIL activity occurs, it should remain proportional and not distract from development.

Junior Year

Focus: Performance peak and projection clarity.
Recruiting relevance: High. Most meaningful recruiting conversations occur here.
NIL relevance: May increase if visibility grows through performance.

This is where discipline pays off.

Senior Year

Focus: Fit, decision-making, academic planning.
Recruiting relevance: Finalization.
NIL relevance: Supplemental.

Momentum should follow performance — not precede it.

Remember: Understanding this arc reduces panic. Recruiting is rarely a race at age twelve.

Part II — The Business of Exposure

If recruiting were only about performance, the landscape would be quiet. It isn't.

Because recruiting now intersects with media, technology, subscription platforms, event operators, scouting databases, and marketing companies. That intersection creates opportunity — and noise. Families are not just navigating college coaches anymore. They are navigating an ecosystem. Understanding that ecosystem reduces vulnerability.

Myth #4: A Recruiting Service Guarantees Access

FILM ROOM

Let's return to Caleb's $1,495 email. After the emotional surge passed, his father began to evaluate the offer.

The company promised:

- A professionally designed recruiting profile
- Distribution to hundreds of college programs
- Social media amplification
- "Direct coach visibility"

What does "distribution" actually mean? In many cases, it means inclusion in a digital database. In some cases, it means a mass email blast. And in rare cases, it includes targeted outreach based on fit. Those are very different services.

College coaches do not recruit based on email volume. They recruit based on need and evaluation. If a coach needs a left-handed pitcher who can consistently throw in the upper 80s, a mass-distributed profile does not override radar gun reality.

Families should ask:

- How many actual responses do clients receive?
- What percentage of clients receive offers?
- What sports and levels are most successful?
- Is there verification?

If answers are anecdotal or evasive, that should tell you something. Some recruiting services do provide value. They may:

- Help organize communication
- Track outreach
- Provide video editing support
- Offer honest evaluation feedback

Those are structural tools, but structure is different from guarantees. No legitimate recruiting service can promise an offer. If they do, walk away.

Myth #5: Showcases Automatically Increase Recruitment

Showcases are emotionally powerful environments. Athletes compete in front of dozens of evaluators. Parents see clipboards. Cameras. Logos on polos. It all feels official.

But not all showcases operate the same way. Let's examine two scenarios.

Scenario A: Targeted Showcase

An athlete attends a regional event aligned with their realistic level of play. Confirmed attending programs match that level. The athlete performs competitively. Follow-up communication occurs.

This is productive exposure.

Scenario B: Prestige Showcase

An athlete attends a high-profile national event far above their current projection. Hundreds of athletes compete. Evaluation time is limited. The athlete gains experience but recruiting movement is minimal.

The event was not harmful. It simply did not align with current readiness.

The key question before registering for any showcase is: Does this event align with where my athlete realistically projects today?

Exposure without alignment is expensive repetition.

Myth #6: Scholarship = Full Ride

This myth persists because the phrase "scholarship" sounds definitive. In reality, scholarship structures vary dramatically by sport and division. In many sports:

- Scholarships are divided among multiple athletes.
- Coaches distribute partial awards strategically.
- Academic aid is blended with athletic aid.
- Renewal is annual, not guaranteed.

For example:

- A coach may have 11 scholarships to distribute across a 30+ athlete roster. That requires division.
- Full scholarships exist in some sports more commonly than others. But they are not universal.
- The probability of competing at the NCAA Division I level is limited.
- The probability of receiving a full athletic scholarship is smaller still.

That reality is not discouraging. It is grounding.

When families understand scholarship distribution early, they:

- Keep academic performance central.
- Evaluate financial planning realistically.
- Avoid over-investing in exposure purchases.
- Broaden definition of success.

Division II, Division III, NAIA, and junior college pathways all provide meaningful opportunities. Recruiting success is not one uniform outcome.

Myth #7: Social Media Following Impresses Coaches

In a previous chapter, we discussed digital presence. Here's the reality: coaches may glance at social media, but they evaluate film.

A 20,000-follower account does not override foot speed, arm strength, or positional awareness. In fact, over-curated branding without corresponding performance can create doubt. Authenticity and discipline matter.

If social media enhances professionalism, it helps. But if it becomes distraction, it hinders. NIL and recruiting can coexist, but they should not compete for attention.

The Psychology of Urgency

Recruiting services and exposure platforms operate within a psychological window.

- Right after a breakout game
- Right after a tournament win
- Right after a ranking update

Emotion is high, decision-making is compressed. Urgency marketing is not inherently unethical, but families should recognize it.

Phrases like:

- "Limited time opportunity."
- "Selected prospect."
- "Exclusive invitation."

are designed to accelerate commitment.

Where NIL Actually Fits

NIL does not drive recruiting for most high school athletes.
But it can develop skills that indirectly help:

- Professional communication
- Time management
- Financial literacy
- Brand awareness
- Personal responsibility

Those are maturity markers. Coaches value maturity. But the value comes from behavior, not from sponsorship logos.

If NIL begins to dominate time or identity before recruiting readiness is established, priorities may blur.

A Second Story: The Slow Build

FILM ROOM

Emily was a junior soccer player who had not received major recruiting attention by mid-season. Her teammates were announcing visits online. Parents were talking in the stands. Comparison crept in. Instead of purchasing a broad recruiting package, Emily's family took a narrower approach.

They:

- Identified realistic target programs
- Reviewed roster needs
- Sent concise introduction emails

- Included updated game film
- Followed up respectfully

They also continued strength training and skill development. In February, a Division II coach responded. In March, a visit occurred. In April, an offer was extended.

- No exposure blast.
- No urgency purchase.
- No mass distribution.

Just alignment, readiness, and disciplined communication. Recruiting is rarely cinematic, but it is often methodical.

A Healthier Recruiting Framework

Instead of chasing noise, families can anchor to a steadier model:

- Prioritize development
- Understand realistic projection
- Build a clean film library
- Communicate directly
- Follow up respectfully
- Align exposure with readiness
- Keep academics strong
- Evaluate services critically
- Maintain emotional balance

This framework does not guarantee an offer, nothing does. But it reduces regret.

An Empowered Perspective

Recruiting culture can feel like acceleration. But most successful recruiting journeys feel more like progression.

- Steady improvement
- Clear communication
- Measured decisions

NIL should not distort that progression. The athletes who thrive are rarely the loudest early, they are the most prepared when the right coach looks.

And that distinction changes everything.

The Cost Reality No One Talks About

Let's slow this down even further.

Families often spend thousands of dollars in the name of recruiting:

- Showcase fees
- Travel costs
- Recruiting platforms
- Video editing services
- Profile subscriptions
- Camps
- Private evaluations

None of these are automatically wrong. But very few families calculate total investment against probable outcome.

Imagine a family spends:

- $1,500 on a recruiting package
- $2,000 on travel showcases
- $800 on profile subscriptions
- $1,200 on specialty camps

That is $5,500.

If the athlete earns a partial scholarship worth $4,000 per year, the math may still make sense. But if no scholarship materializes, and the athlete attends a school primarily for academic reasons, the recruiting investment becomes emotional — not financial — return.

Again, this is not discouragement. It is proportionality.

Recruiting is an opportunity pursuit, not a guaranteed return on investment. When families track expenses honestly, decision-making becomes calmer.

Division Matters More Than Status

Another myth quietly operating in recruiting culture is that Division I is the only "successful" outcome.

The truth:

- Division I rosters are limited.
- Division II programs are competitive and offer athletic aid.
- Division III programs offer no athletic scholarships but often provide strong academic packages.
- NAIA programs provide opportunities across many sports.
- Junior colleges offer development pathways.

The level of play is not always correlated with personal growth or long-term success. Families who broaden their definition of success reduce unnecessary pressure.

Fit often matters more than logo.

Recruiting Services

Let's examine two families.

Family A

Purchases a $2,000 recruiting package.

Receives:

- A polished digital profile
- Mass email distribution
- Social media graphics
- Access to a large database

They assume outreach has been handled, so they wait. Minimal direct communication occurs.

Family B

Spends $0 on a package.

They:

- Research 20 target schools.
- Study rosters.
- Identify positional needs.
- Draft personalized emails.
- Attach updated film.

- Follow up every 4–6 weeks.

They track responses. They adjust.

Which family is more likely to receive meaningful engagement? The answer is not always Family B. But disciplined direct communication often produces clearer outcomes than passive distribution.

Recruiting rewards initiative, not subscription status.

The Panic Spiral

Recruiting anxiety rarely appears all at once. It builds gradually and starts with comparison:

- A teammate announces an offer.
- A social media post highlights a commitment.
- A ranking is published.
- Parents talk in the stands.

Then questions emerge:

- "Should we be doing more?"
- "Are we behind?"
- "What if we missed something?"

That internal spiral often leads to reactive purchases. When families operate from panic, evaluation declines. The antidote is information.

When you understand:

- Recruiting timelines
- Scholarship distribution

- Probability
- Development curves

you interrupt panic with perspective. This greatly stabilizes decisions.

When Branding Distorts Recruiting

Occasionally, NIL ambition outruns recruiting reality.

An athlete builds an elaborate brand presence early.

- Logos
- Custom graphics
- Merchandise drops
- Aggressive monetization posts

Meanwhile, performance plateaus.

College coaches evaluating film may quietly note the imbalance. Doing this branding is not inherently negative, but branding without corresponding development can signal misaligned priorities.

NIL should enhance maturity, not overshadow improvement.

The Math of Visibility

Let's revisit the idea that "more exposure equals more opportunity."

If a coach receives 500 prospect emails in a month and has 3 roster spots to fill, volume does not change scarcity. Their recruiting remains selective. Visibility does not eliminate evaluation thresholds.

This is why aligning exposure with realistic projection matters.

- Right place.
- Right time.
- Right level.

That equation beats volume.

Final Reflection

Recruiting is competitive. You already know this. It is also structured. It is not random, mystical, or solved by urgency.

If there is one principle to carry forward from this chapter, it is this:

- Exposure should follow readiness.
- NIL should follow performance.
- Decisions should follow information.

When families operate from that posture, recruiting becomes manageable.

Visibility vs. Value

FILM ROOM

When Liam crossed 40,000 followers, his phone lit up with congratulatory messages.

Teammates commented with fire emojis. A local training account reposted one of his highlights. His profile looked polished: branded graphics, edited film, and motivational captions. His parents had invested in a videographer. They had learned how to schedule posts at optimal times. Engagement was steady.

From the outside, momentum seemed obvious. Inside the recruiting process, very little changed.

Analytics showed only two coaches viewed his profile. One had sent a generic camp invitation. There were no sustained conversations, no requests for updated film, no roster discussions. The family's confusion was understandable. If he was visible, why wasn't he converting?

That question sits at the center of modern youth sports culture. We have built an environment where visibility feels like advancement. The athlete who is seen appears to be moving forward. The athlete who is quiet appears to be falling behind. But visibility and value are not interchangeable.

Amplification without substance fades quickly. Substance without amplification eventually gets noticed.

Why Visibility Feels Productive

There is a psychological reason visibility is so seductive. Posting content feels active. Attending high-profile events feels active. Announcing offers, even unofficial interest, feels like movement. These actions create the sensation that something is happening. And in recruiting culture, inactivity feels dangerous.

When other families are posting commitments, campus visits, and ranking updates, silence can feel like stagnation. Parents worry that if they are not consistently visible, coaches will forget about their athlete. But college coaches do not build recruiting boards based on which athletes post the most frequently. They build recruiting boards based on roster construction, measurable data, projection curves, and positional need.

Visibility may bring a coach's eyes to film once. It does not create a second evaluation unless the underlying performance warrants it.

The same principle applies to NIL. A brand may notice an athlete's following. But if engagement is shallow or inconsistent, the opportunity rarely develops beyond an initial inquiry.

Attention and leverage are different currencies.

What Recruiting Actually Rewards

Recruiting is fundamentally an evaluation system. Coaches study film to answer specific questions:

- Does this athlete help us compete at our level?
- Does this athlete project physically over the next three years?

- Does this athlete fit our tactical system?
- Can this athlete handle the academic expectations of our institution?

None of those questions are answered by follower count. They are answered by film quality, game impact, consistency, coach feedback, and academic transcripts.

An athlete with modest online presence but strong measurable growth, improved speed, improved strength, improved efficiency, will consistently generate more sustained recruiting interest than an athlete with heavy digital presence and plateaued development.

Visibility can create a first impression, but value sustains it.

What NIL Actually Rewards

NIL introduces a separate evaluation model, but the same distinction applies. Brands are not looking for popularity alone. They are looking for alignment and for sales.

For a local business, 5,000 highly engaged local followers can be more valuable than 40,000 disengaged accounts scattered across the country. Engagement rate, trust, credibility, and reliability often matter more than scale.

A high school athlete who communicates professionally, shows up on time, delivers agreed content, and maintains authenticity creates brand confidence.

That confidence is value. The number attached to the account is visibility.

Without engagement and credibility, visibility is hollow.

The "Personal Brand at Fifteen" Conversation

The phrase "build your brand" has filtered into youth sports so thoroughly that it is now used in middle school gyms. The intention is usually positive. Families want to support their athletes. They want to teach responsibility and entrepreneurship.

But there is a sequencing issue that often goes unexamined.

A brand is an external expression of internal substance. If the internal substance, performance, discipline, emotional maturity, is still forming, an aggressive external brand can create imbalance. Public persona begins to outpace private development.

When that happens, pressure increases. Identity becomes performance-dependent in a different way. The athlete begins managing perception before mastering craft. There is nothing wrong with teaching professionalism early. There is risk in constructing a public identity before the foundation is steady.

In most cases, brand should follow value.

A Quieter Example

FILM ROOM

Sophia's social media presence was clean but minimal. She posted occasional game clips and team photos. No custom logos. No merchandise. No elaborate content calendar. What she did consistently was improve.

Her strength numbers increased each year. Her game impact became more measurable. Her coaches described her as reliable and coachable. Her academics remained strong.

By junior spring, she had three meaningful recruiting conversations underway. Later that summer, a local training facility approached her about promoting its youth camps. The facility owner had watched her compete and trusted her credibility in the community.

Her NIL opportunity did not create her recruiting interest, but it did create an opportunity.

Measurable Growth vs. Marketable Appearance

There are two categories families should distinguish clearly.

Measurable growth includes:

- Speed improvements
- Strength progression
- Skill refinement
- Game efficiency
- Consistency under pressure
- Academic reliability

Marketable appearance includes:

- Graphic design
- Follower count
- Posting frequency
- Branding aesthetics

Both can coexist. But one drives outcomes more reliably.

A polished profile cannot compensate for stagnant development.

Conversely, steady development eventually forces attention, even if branding is modest. College coaches recruit athletes who project forward. Brands partner with athletes who influence authentically. In both cases, substance outweighs surface.

The Engagement Illusion

Let's talk about engagement math, because this is where visibility often collapses under scrutiny.

An athlete has 40,000 followers. This sounds impressive.

But look closer.

If the average post receives:

- 1,200 likes
- 20 comments
- Minimal saves or shares

The engagement rate is roughly 3%. In social media terms, that is moderate.

Now compare that to an athlete with 5,000 followers whose posts regularly receive:

- 600 likes
- 50 comments
- High local interaction

That engagement rate is closer to 12–15%.

For a local business deciding whether to invest $1,000 in a promotional partnership. The second athlete is often more valuable because influence is not about audience size, it is about audience response.

The same principle applies to recruiting visibility.

A coach viewing film is not impressed by the volume of posts, they are evaluating efficiency, decision-making, and mechanics, projection. If the film is strong, it does not need weekly re-posting to convert. If film is weak, no amount of reposting improves it.

The Visibility Trap

There is a subtle trap that develops when visibility becomes the priority. This is: athletes begin to optimize for what performs online.

- Highlight plays
- Big reactions
- Emotionally charged moments

Meanwhile, the habits that create long-term improvement such as defensive positioning, conditioning, discipline, and repetition receive less attention because they do not trend. This shifts focus.

Instead of asking, "What helps me improve?" the athlete may unconsciously begin asking, "What looks good?" That shift is small, but over time, it compounds.

Coaches evaluate habits. Social media rewards moments.

If an athlete trains for moments instead of habits, recruiting value erodes even as visibility increases.

A Coach's Perspective

Imagine sitting inside a college coaching office in October.

There are:

- Hundreds of emails
- Film links
- Roster gaps to fill
- Budget constraints
- Academic standards
- Character evaluations

A coach may glance at an athlete's social media presence out of curiosity. They may notice professionalism or immaturity. But they do not allocate scholarship dollars based on branding aesthetics. They allocate based on roster math.

- Can this athlete fill a position we are losing next year?
- Does this athlete project physically over three years?
- Does this athlete compete at our level of speed and strength?
- Does this athlete's coach speak highly of their work ethic?

Those variables convert.

Visibility may introduce the athlete, but value determines whether the conversation continues.

The Brand Inflation Problem

In the NIL environment, another issue emerges: brand inflation. Athletes see professional players launch clothing lines and assume replication is strategic. But professional athletes build brands on established performance credibility.

When high school athletes attempt to scale branding beyond their current value, two risks emerge: financial risk and identity risk.

Merchandise drops that do not convert create discouragement. Heavy branding without deal flow creates imbalance. Identity risk is subtler. If an athlete's identity becomes centered on being "a brand" before performance stabilizes, external validation becomes central.

When performance dips, as it inevitably does at some point, confidence becomes fragile.

Now, this is not an argument against ambition, it is an argument for sequencing.

The Compound Value Model

Let's build a model that contrasts two pathways.

Path A: Visibility First

Year 1:

- Aggressive branding
- Frequent posting
- Showcase-heavy schedule

Year 2:

- Similar performance metrics
- Increased follower count
- Minimal recruiting movement

Year 3:

- Fatigue
- Pressure
- Confusion about stagnation

Path B: Value First

Year 1:

- Strength training
- Skill refinement
- Film improvement

Year 2:

- Measurable growth
- Increased coach communication
- Modest, authentic digital presence

Year 3:

- Recruiting leverage
- Credible NIL inquiries
- Clear identity rooted in performance

The second path feels slower early but accelerates later. The first path feels faster early but often plateaus. Families must decide which curve they prefer.

The Parent Role in the Visibility Equation

Parents often unintentionally accelerate the visibility push. They want to advocate, help, and when they see other families posting graphics and announcements they assume they are falling behind.

It is natural.

But when parents become marketing managers before they become development partners, priorities can shift.

The more effective parental role often looks like:

- Tracking strength progression
- Encouraging academic discipline
- Monitoring sleep and recovery
- Supporting communication habits
- Maintaining perspective

These do not trend online; they create leverage offline.

When Visibility Becomes Leverage

There is a point at which visibility and value align. An athlete with strong performance metrics, consistent film, and positive coach feedback may reach a tipping point.

At that stage:

- Recruiting interest increases.
- NIL inquiries become more organic.
- Media mentions occur naturally.

Exposure amplifies credibility rather than substitutes for it. Visibility becomes leverage when it rests on substance.

A Realignment Question

Instead of asking: "How do we grow?"

Ask:

- "In what measurable ways have we improved this year?"
- If speed has not improved.
- If strength has plateaued.
- If film looks similar to last season.
- If communication habits remain inconsistent.

Then visibility is unlikely to convert.

Recruiting and NIL both respond to progress that is quantifiable. Followers are visible. They are not always correlated.

When Visibility Helps

Visibility is not the problem. It becomes powerful when layered onto real value. If film is strong, visibility accelerates discovery. If engagement is authentic, visibility increases conversion. If communication is disciplined, visibility amplifies opportunity.

The mistake is not being visible; it is confusing visibility with progress. When families ask, "How do we get seen more?" they often skip the more important question: "Are we improving in ways that matter?" Improvement is slower. It is less glamorous.

A More Stable Model

Instead of building strategy around attention, build it around improvement. Recruiting momentum grows when performance peaks at the right time. NIL momentum grows when credibility and engagement align. That rhythm is steadier than chasing trends.

Families who prioritize measurable growth over constant amplification often feel less frantic. Their decisions become grounded in evidence rather than comparison. Over time, value compounds. Improvement builds leverage. Leverage creates options. Options reduce pressure, and when pressure decreases, clarity improves.

Recruiting and NIL both reward clarity more than noise.

Case Study: When Visibility Outpaces Readiness

FILM ROOM

Marcus entered his junior year with momentum.

He had invested heavily in presentation. A videographer followed him through offseason workouts. His Instagram featured cinematic edits — slow-motion cuts, dramatic music, motivational captions. He launched personal merchandise with a logo that blended his initials into a sleek emblem.

By mid-season, he had 28,000 followers. But something else was happening quietly.

His measurable performance metrics had not changed significantly from the previous year. His 40-yard-dash time remained flat. His in-game efficiency was inconsistent. His decision-making under pressure had not stabilized.

College coaches watched film. They did not comment on graphics. They noted footwork inconsistencies. They noted hesitation reads. They noted projection questions.

Marcus began to feel confused. "They're seeing me," he told his parents. "Why aren't they offering?" Simple, because visibility had increased and value had not.

This is not a condemnation of ambition. Marcus was working hard. But effort was directed disproportionately toward amplification rather than measurable growth.

Midway through the season, a trusted mentor suggested something simple: "What if the next six months are about improvement no one can post?"

The following spring, his measurable metrics improved significantly. Recruiting communication shifted. Interest became specific. The visibility returned later, but this time it rested on substance.

The lesson is not to avoid visibility; it is to avoid confusing amplification with acceleration.

Inside a College Recruiting Room

Picture a coaching staff in February.

Whiteboard filled with position depth charts. Returning seniors marked in red. Projected graduations circled. Budget columns outlining scholarship distribution.

An assistant coach opens a recruiting database. He filters by position, height range, academic GPA, geographic preference. A list populates. He clicks on film.

The evaluation begins within seconds:

- Does the athlete move fluidly?
- Is the first step explosive?
- Is decision-making fast?
- Does effort persist late in games?
- Is there upward trajectory compared to older clips?

The assistant coach does not scroll Instagram first, he watches game film. If the film answers questions positively, the athlete moves into the "re-evaluate" column. If it does not, the file closes.

The decision is rarely emotional.

Recruiting boards operate on projection curves, not popularity curves. Understanding that environment removes much of the mystique. Coaches are not ignoring visibility, they are prioritizing need.

Announcement Culture vs Development Culture

We now live in an announcement culture.

- Offer graphics.
- Commitment videos.
- Top-10 school lists.
- Ranking updates.

These announcements create the illusion that recruiting is constant momentum. What is rarely posted are the months between.

- The repetition.
- The plateau.
- The strength cycles.
- The academic grind.
- The private doubts.

Development culture is quieter and values:

- Incremental improvement
- Process discipline
- Patience
- Honest evaluation
- Coach feedback

Announcement culture rewards moments. Development culture rewards progression.

If an athlete's identity becomes tethered to announcements, the absence of news feels like failure. If identity is tethered to improvement, silence feels like preparation. Families must decide which culture they want to participate in.

One produces short bursts of attention, the other produces durable leverage.

The NIL Overlay

In the NIL era, announcement culture intensifies. Brand deals are announced publicly. Partnerships are shared widely. Followers track growth in real time. That transparency and immediacy can distort perception. An athlete may believe if they are not securing visible deals, they are missing out.

But NIL, like recruiting, follows value more often than it creates it.

A local business partnering with a high school athlete usually asks:

- Is this athlete respected in the community?
- Is their audience engaged?
- Are they reliable?

Those questions mirror recruiting questions. Credibility precedes compensation. If development doesn't progress, while branding escalates, the athlete's overall foundation weakens. If development deepens while branding remains proportional, this can create opportunity.

A Reframing Exercise

When evaluating strategy, ask three questions:

- What measurable performance improvements occurred this year?
- What meaningful recruiting conversations have progressed this year?
- What authentic NIL opportunities emerged organically this year?

If the answer to the first question is unclear, focus there. If the second question lacks traction, examine film and projection. If the third question feels forced, reassess engagement and credibility.

Progress is rarely simultaneous across all three. But performance improvement remains the most controllable variable.

Long-Term Leverage

Visibility spikes. Value compounds. This compounding works slowly at first.

- Strength gains accumulate.
- Decision-making sharpens.
- Game awareness stabilizes.
- Academic reliability builds trust.

Over time, that compounding creates leverage creating options. Families who prioritize leverage over attention tend to experience fewer dramatic swings. Their athletes grow steadily.

Their NIL opportunities feel aligned rather than rushed and their recruiting conversations feel earned rather than chased.

A Practical Audit: Are We Building Visibility or Value?

Every season, families make dozens of small decisions shaping direction. Most of them do not feel dramatic at the moment. They are scheduling, budget, and time decisions. But over time, those small decisions reveal priority. If you are unsure whether your strategy is tilted toward visibility or value, conduct a simple audit. Here are some ideas:

1. Where Is the Majority of Time Going?

Track one month honestly.

How many hours were spent on:

- Skill development and training?
- Strength and conditioning?
- Studying film?
- Recovery time and sleep?
- Social media posting and editing?
- Graphic design or announcement preparation?
- Showcase travel primarily for exposure?

There is no universal correct ratio. But if the hours devoted to presentation consistently exceed the hours devoted to development, the imbalance will eventually surface. Recruiting boards do not reward aesthetic polish over athletic progression.

2. What Has Actually Improved?

At the end of each season, list measurable changes.

- Speed times
- Strength numbers

- Shooting percentages
- Tackle efficiency
- Assist-to-turnover ratio
- Academic GPA
- Coach evaluations

If those numbers are moving upward, then the athlete's value is compounding. If they are flat year after year, adding more visibility rarely solves the issue.

3. Would This Strategy Make Sense Without Social Media?

This question strips away noise. If there were no platforms, no public announcements, no follower counts — would you still be investing in the same camps, the same training, the same schedule?
If the answer is yes, the strategy is likely development driven. If the answer is no, it may be presentation driven.

4. Is Attention Creating Pressure?

When attention increases, stress often increases with it.

Is your athlete feeling energized by growth, or anxious about maintaining image? Are conversations at home centered on improvement, or on comparisons?

Visibility that strengthens confidence is healthy but visibility that creates performance anxiety should be recalibrated.

5. If a Coach Asked, "Why Should I Recruit You?," What Is the Answer?

The answer should not begin with a social media follower count; it should begin with performance value:

- "I compete at this level."

- "I've improved in these measurable ways."
- "My coaches describe me as reliable and disciplined."
- "My academic record shows consistency."

Visibility can supplement that answer, it should not replace it.

The Long Game

High school athletics are brief. Development arcs are not.

An athlete who builds strength, discipline, emotional maturity, and consistency during these years carries those traits forward whether recruiting accelerates or not. An athlete who builds only visibility carries fewer durable assets. Their attention fades, their work ethic erodes. Confidence rooted in improvement survives transition while confidence rooted in attention fluctuates.

When families evaluate strategy through that lens, decisions become clearer.

Closing Perspective

Visibility definitely has a role. It introduces, amplifies, and accelerates. But this introduction is not conversion. Acceleration without foundation leads to instability.

When performance growth leads and visibility follows, both recruiting and NIL become more predictable. That predictability does not eliminate competition, but it does ease confusion.

Families who build value first often find attention arrives at the right time, not because they chase it relentlessly, but because they were ready when the opportunity presented itself.

Digital Presence Done Responsibly

FILM ROOM

The post was live for six minutes.

Marc, a sophomore basketball player, talented and nationally ranked in his age group, reposted a meme mocking an opposing player after a weekend tournament. It wasn't overtly vulgar or threatening. It was sarcastic and dismissive, the kind of thing teenagers share without much thought.

Within minutes, someone screenshotted it. Within an hour, it circulated through group chats. By the next morning, a recruiting coordinator from a mid-major program had seen it. Marc deleted the post quickly. His parents spoke with him about sportsmanship. The situation never became a public blowup. There was no viral controversy, no formal discipline, no headlines.

But something subtle shifted.

The coaching staff never brought it up directly. They simply cooled communication. The follow-up calls became less frequent. The tone changed.

Was that one post the sole reason? Probably not. Recruiting decisions are rarely that simple. But recruiting is built on cumulative impressions, and coaches aren't only projecting physical development. They're projecting maturity, stability, and cultural fit.

Digital presence has become part of that projection.

What Actually Happened After the Six-Minute Post

Marc never received a formal reprimand from the recruiting coordinator. There was no confrontation. But inside the program's recruiting database, his profile was adjusted. When assistants revisit prospects throughout the year, they make short notes. These notes are not dramatic. They are often one line. But those lines accumulate.

The athlete's file included updated film grades, athletic metrics, academic GPA, and coach feedback.

And one additional line: "Monitor social maturity."

That phrase did not remove him from the board. It did something more subtle. It made him a slightly riskier projection. Recruiting at the college level is about stacking small advantages. When two athletes appear similar athletically, staff lean toward the safer cultural fit. One impulsive digital moment rarely ends a recruitment, but recruiting is rarely lost in one dramatic event. It drifts.

Calls become less frequent. Evaluations slow. Priority shifts. Marc and his family never knew why communication cooled.

That uncertainty is what makes digital responsibility important. You often will not know when a post altered perception.

A Digital Timeline: How Responsibility Changes by Grade

Families sometimes ask, "At what age does this really matter?" The answer is gradual.

Middle School (6th–8th Grade)

The recruiting impact is minimal. The reputational foundation is not.

At this stage:

- Parents should actively supervise
- Accounts should be private
- Safety settings should be confirmed
- Public controversy should be avoided entirely

This is training ground, not branding ground.

Freshman Year

Recruiting begins quietly in some sports.

Digital presence should shift toward:

- Clean game clips
- Team acknowledgement
- Academic balance
- Zero opponent commentary

No urgency exists to build a "brand." Development remains primary.

Sophomore Year

Now coaches begin casual digital reviews.

This is when:

- Offer announcements must be accurate
- Tone matters
- Group chat discipline matters
- Public maturity begins to separate athletes

Junior Year

This is the most sensitive digital year. Recruiting decisions accelerate. NIL inquiries may begin locally.

At this stage:

- Emotional discipline must be established
- NIL content must remain proportionate
- Political and controversial commentary should be approached carefully
- Professional tone in DMs becomes essential

Senior Year

By now, digital habits are established.

If recruiting is complete, the focus shifts toward:

- Transition readiness
- Maintaining reputation
- Preparing for increased independence

Digital responsibility is developmental and scales with exposure.

Political Commentary and Public Opinion

This section requires balance. High school athletes are citizens. They have opinions. They are not required to be silent on every issue.

However, families should understand two realities:

- College programs are risk-sensitive environments.
- Public commentary lives permanently.

Coaches recruit into team ecosystems with donors, alumni, administrators, and diverse teammates. Highly polarizing digital behavior can introduce friction—even when intentions are sincere. This does not mean athletes must avoid all opinion, but it does mean:

- Avoid reactionary posting.
- Avoid inflammatory tone.
- Avoid attacking individuals.
- Consider long-term projection.

A thoughtful, measured post is very different from an impulsive rant. The issue is not belief. It is volatility.

NIL Professionalism: What Brands Quietly Track

When NIL grows beyond one small local deal, brands begin to watch patterns.

They evaluate:

- Posting consistency
- Response time to emails

- Reliability in meeting deadlines
- Clarity in captions
- Absence of controversy

An athlete may believe their performance is the primary value driver. For brands, reliability is often equally important. A high school athlete who misses posting deadlines or responds inconsistently may quietly lose renewal opportunities. Digital professionalism is not about polish; it is about dependability.

The Emotional Delay Rule

Most digital mistakes happen during emotional spikes.

- After a win
- After a loss
- After a controversial call
- After a recruiting disappointment

A simple structural safeguard prevents most problems. Create a 24-hour rule for emotionally charged posts. If something feels intense, draft it. Save it. Revisit the next day. Most posts lose urgency overnight, emotional delay protects reputation.

Digital Presence Is Now Part of Evaluation

College coaches look at social media. Not all of them, not obsessively, and not as a primary evaluation tool—but often enough that families should assume it will be seen. Most coaches aren't scanning for follower count first. They are scanning for risk and tone. They're looking for red flags such as:

- Public disrespect toward opponents, officials, or teammates

- Inflammatory or polarizing content that suggests poor judgment
- Evidence of substance misuse or reckless behavior
- Aggressive conflict, threats, bullying, or humiliation content
- Patterns of immaturity that suggest volatility

They also notice something subtle: how the athlete carries themselves.

- Is the account consistently self-promotional?
- Does it reflect team awareness or only personal branding?
- Does the athlete argue in comments?
- Do they handle criticism with composure or defensiveness?

Digital presence does not win scholarships. It can quietly lose them.

The Screenshot Effect

After that six-minute post circulated, no coach called to scold Marc. No one "caught" him in a dramatic way. The recruiting coordinator simply added a quiet note to the file. "Emotional volatility online — monitor." That note didn't eliminate Marc. It just added friction.

Recruiting boards are crowded. When two prospects look similar on film, staff look for separators. Sometimes the separator is upside. Sometimes it's academic stability. Sometimes it's coachability, and sometimes it's perceived risk.

Marc never knew a short-lived post changed how he was viewed. That's common. Most recruiting shifts happen quietly. Digital presence is rarely dramatic in its impact; it's cumulative.

A key idea to hold onto: deletion is not erasure. Screenshots, re-shares, archives, and private forwarding can preserve content even after it's removed.

A Near Miss That Almost Cost a Deal

FILM ROOM

Tyler, a junior baseball player, had built a clean and professional online presence. His following was modest, but local engagement was strong. He didn't post controversy and he didn't stir conflict.

A local sports performance gym approached him for a small NIL deal: two posts per month and an appearance at a youth clinic. The agreement was simple and compensation was reasonable. The owner valued Tyler's credibility, especially with younger athletes in the community.

One week before the announcement, Tyler reposted a viral video mocking a rival team's player who had committed elsewhere. It was meant as humor. His friends reacted positively.

The gym owner called the next morning.

"We're about to position you as a leader for our younger athletes," he said. "That repost doesn't align with the image we're building."

The deal didn't disappear, but it did pause. Tyler removed the repost and clarified his intent. It felt awkward and overblown to him, until he realized the bigger lesson: Brands evaluate character as much as reach. Recruiting evaluates projection as much as talent. A single post doesn't define an athlete, but it can introduce doubt, and doubt reduces leverage.

Where Oversight Becomes Protection

Parents often struggle with the balance between control and autonomy.

If you monitor too closely, you risk undermining trust. If you ignore everything, you leave preventable mistakes on the table. The most effective approach is usually conversational, not authoritarian. Instead of demanding passwords, consider establishing shared expectations, simple standards your child agrees to follow:

- No posting during emotional spikes (wins, losses, conflicts)
- No commentary about officials or opponents
- No public airing of team conflict
- No announcing "offers" until the athlete has clarity and confirmation
- No tagging coaches repeatedly for attention

These aren't rules meant to suppress personality. They're guardrails meant to preserve opportunity. Teenagers don't always perceive long-term consequences. That isn't a moral failure; it's developmental reality. Calm guidance reduces reputational drift.

The Problem With "Offer Graphics" and Inflation

One of the most common credibility issues online is premature announcement culture.

A coach says, "Stay in touch." Another says, "We'd like you at camp." Another says, "We're evaluating you." Those can be meaningful signs of interest, but they aren't always the same as an offer. Within hours, sometimes a graphic appears: "Blessed to receive an offer."

Sometimes it's accurate. Sometimes it stretches interpretation.

Coaches notice.

Recruiting staff communicates internally. When an athlete publicly announces something that doesn't align with the program's documentation, credibility erodes. It may not end recruiting interest, but it creates friction that didn't need to exist. Honest communication builds trust. Inflated posts create correction moments.

Group Chats and Collateral Risk

Digital presence is not limited to public posts. Private group chats generate some of the most damaging screenshots:

- Complaints about coaching
- Mockery of opponents
- Inside jokes that look cruel out of context
- Frustration that becomes personal

These conversations feel insulated until they aren't. When conflict arises inside a team, screenshots travel. When transfers happen, history surfaces. When recruiting heats up, competitors look for advantage. Private does not mean safe. Even in "friends only" spaces, foresight matters. Character is consistent across contexts.

Mental Health and the Comparison Cycle

Digital platforms amplify comparison. Athletes scroll and see commitment videos, offer graphics, highlight reels, NIL partnerships, and ranking updates. Without context, it can look like constant advancement.

Parents often underestimate how much this affects teenagers. If visibility becomes a scoreboard, self-worth can become tied to engagement. Low engagement can feel like rejection. Silence can feel like failure.

Responsible digital presence includes boundaries:

- Periodic breaks during high-pressure seasons
- Reducing algorithm exposure during recruiting lulls
- Offline focus windows that prioritize training, recovery, and school

Stability matters more than constant exposure.

Parents, Authenticity, and Outsourcing

Families generally fall into three models when it comes to social media:
Athlete-run

- Parent-assisted
- Outsourced to a third party
- Each has trade-offs.

Athlete-run

This is the most authentic model and builds maturity. The risk is impulsivity, especially after emotional events. Parental involvement works best as coaching and conversation, not surveillance.

Parent-assisted

This can provide structure, especially earlier in high school. The risk is tone. Coaches can often sense when an account feels adult-managed or overly curated, which can reduce authenticity.

Outsourced

Outsourcing is increasingly common. It isn't inherently wrong, but it can create imbalance if the brand outpaces the athlete's performance credibility. If families outsource, the goal should be to enhance clarity and consistency, not inflate image.

A simple test helps: if the account no longer sounds like the athlete, it's drifting into performance rather than representation.

Public vs Private Accounts

Making an account private reduces exposure, but it doesn't eliminate risk. Private content can still be screenshotted, forwarded, and recirculated. Public accounts carry greater scrutiny. Private accounts carry a false sense of insulation. Either way, the content should withstand visibility.

Platform Safety Settings and Minor Protections

If the athlete is under 18, safety settings matter. Families should verify platform protections are active, especially on Instagram and similar services.

Instagram, for example, includes teen/child protections and supervised settings that can limit:

- Direct messaging from unknown adults
- Public visibility of contact info
- Certain kinds of unwanted contact or targeting

At minimum, families should check:

- The account's age/teen settings are correct
- Contact information is not publicly exposed
- Location tagging is used cautiously

DM filters and message requests are configured safely
These are not marketing decisions. They are safety decisions.

Direct Messages From Coaches

DMs are increasingly common for initial coach contact. Athletes should treat DMs like professional communication:

- Clear grammar
- Respectful tone
- No slang
- No overfamiliar language
- No emotional replies

If a coach's message is unclear, asking a neutral clarifying question is appropriate. If communication feels inappropriate or unusual, parents should be informed immediately.

DMs leave records. Use that to your advantage.

NIL Requires Professionalism

As NIL opportunities develop, digital professionalism becomes even more important.

Brands tend to value stability and reliability over flash. They look for:

- Timely responses to messages
- Clear communication about deliverables
- Respectful engagement with followers
- Minimal controversy
- Consistency in tone

NIL is not just about exposure. It is about trust. Digital recklessness reduces brand confidence quickly.

A Practical Digital Hygiene Audit

At the beginning of each school year (or each season), do a digital audit:

- Review old posts and archive what no longer reflects growth.
- Update privacy and safety settings.
- Confirm teen/child protections are active.
- Remove contact info from public bio if unnecessary.
- Review tagged photos and remove questionable tags.
- Scan followers for unknown adult accounts and adjust settings if needed.

This is not image manipulation. It's maturation. Your digital footprint should reflect who you are becoming, not who you were at thirteen.

If a Coach Reviewed Your Feed Today

Imagine a college assistant coach opens the athlete's profile right now. What would they see in the first thirty seconds? Coaches are busy. They scan fast. They're looking for signals.

First glance: profile and bio

- Appropriate photo
- Professional bio
- No immature slogans or clutter
- Clear but reasonable contact info

Second glance: content tone

- Competition and training emphasis
- Signs of discipline
- Team awareness
- Limited drama and reactive posting

Third glance: comments

- Respectful interaction
- No arguing
- No defensive escalation
- A community that feels normal, not chaotic

Fourth glance: highlights

- Organized categories
- Evidence of maturity
- No red flags in "behind the scenes" content

The coach doesn't send an email explaining impressions. They file a feeling: steady, reliable, risky, immature, professional. That impression becomes one more data point in a crowded process.

What If There's Already a Problem?

Not every family starts clean. Maybe there are old posts. Maybe something circulated. Maybe a screenshot surfaced. The goal is not perfection; it's course correction.

Responsible recovery usually looks like this:

- Don't panic publicly. Overcorrection creates attention.
- Remove or archive content quietly. Accept that screenshots may exist.
- If necessary, be transparent with coaches. If something already reached recruiting staff, calm honesty can be better than silence.
- Demonstrate growth through consistency. Maturity is proven over time, not in apology posts.
- Reset standards moving forward.

Recruiting staff understand adolescence. They look for patterns more than isolated mistakes. A corrected mistake followed by stability often strengthens credibility.

Digital Presence Extends Beyond Recruiting

Most families think only about recruiting. Digital history extends beyond it: internships, jobs, admissions decisions, professional opportunities. A teenager may not think about a future employer at sixteen. But permanence means sixteen-year-old decisions sometimes reach twenty-four-year-old consequences.

You're not managing an account for this season alone. You're shaping an archive that will be with them forever.

NIL Growth Without Overexposure

As NIL opportunities increase, digital pressure increases. The goal is to scale without turning the account into a billboard.

Practical guardrails help:

- Maintain a healthy ratio of performance content to promotional content
- Avoid stacking sponsored posts back-to-back
- Clearly label partnerships when required
- Continue team-focused content
- Protect offseason periods from constant posting

Audiences sense imbalance quickly. When every post becomes promotional, engagement drops. Sustainable NIL presence feels integrated, not forced.

The Parent Conversation That Matters

At some point, every family should sit down and ask: "What do we want this account to represent—not just this season, but in five years?"

Is it a highlight reel? A résumé? A recruiting tool? A business platform? A personal journal? Clarity reduces impulse. When identity is defined, posting becomes intentional rather than reactive.

Visibility vs. Value: What Actually Moves the Needle

It is easy to confuse visibility with value. Social media makes visibility measurable. Follower count is public. Likes are visible. Views can be tracked. Engagement becomes a scoreboard.

But recruiting staff and brands rarely equate visibility with value in the way families assume.

A high school athlete with 25,000 followers who posts inconsistently, argues in comments, or inflates recruiting language may be less appealing than an athlete with 1,800 followers whose account feels stable, respectful, and authentic.

Visibility gets attention. Value sustains opportunity.

For recruiting staff, value often looks like:

- Composure in communication
- Evidence of coachability
- Team acknowledgment
- Academic balance
- Absence of volatility

For brands, value often looks like:

- Audience trust, not just audience size
- Local credibility
- Consistent tone
- Predictable posting behavior
- Clean reputation

Follower count without maturity does not move the needle as much as families think. In fact, excessive self-promotion can quietly work against an athlete if it suggests imbalance between development and branding. The question families should ask is not, "How do we grow faster?" It is, "Does this account increase trust?" Trust compounds more reliably than visibility.

When digital presence aligns with work ethic, academics, team culture, and emotional steadiness, it becomes an asset. When it feels inflated, chaotic, or overly commercial too early, it creates friction. Most high school athletes will never need a massive platform to secure recruiting opportunities or small local NIL deals.

- They need clarity.
- They need composure.
- They need credibility.

Those traits rarely trend, but they win quietly.

Digital Discipline Is a Competitive Advantage

Families often treat digital responsibility as damage control. It is more powerful than that. In a recruiting environment where most prospects look similar physically on film, differentiation happens in quieter ways. Coaches compare risk profiles. Brands compare reliability. Administrators compare maturity. Digital discipline becomes a competitive advantage.

Consider two athletes with similar measurables and similar highlight film.

Athlete A posts frequently, reacts emotionally after games, announces interest prematurely, and occasionally engages in comment arguments.

Athlete B posts less frequently but more intentionally. No emotional spikes. Accurate recruiting language. Clear team acknowledgment. No unnecessary drama.

Neither athlete is "perfect," but one feels predictable. That predictability reduces stress for coaches. College staff are managing roster balance, alumni pressure, academic compliance, and internal culture. When they evaluate prospects, they are asking a quiet question: "Will this athlete create additional work?" Digital volatility suggests potential distraction. Digital steadiness suggests cultural fit.

The same principle applies to NIL.

Brands that partner with high school athletes are not only purchasing exposure. They are associating their name with a person. If controversy appears, even minor controversy, the brand absorbs it. A steady digital presence signals low risk. That low risk builds confidence and in turn that confidence renews deals.

The Long View

High school feels immediate. Recruiting feels urgent. NIL can feel both exciting and time sensitive. But a teenager's digital history outlasts all of it. Four years from now, most of the specific posts from this season will not matter.

The reputation pattern will.

- Was this athlete known as steady or reactive?
- Was their account consistent or chaotic?
- Did they represent their team well?
- Did they handle disappointment with maturity?

These patterns become part of how coaches and administrators remember them. Digital presence is not separate from character. It is one more expression of it. Families who understand this rarely need dramatic corrections later.

Closing Perspective

Digital platforms are tools. They can showcase growth, support recruiting communication, and create NIL opportunities. But they are not neutral. They record, distribute, and preserve.

Families who treat digital presence as an extension of character, rather than an extension of hype, tend to navigate recruiting and NIL more smoothly. Responsibility online mirrors responsibility in training: both build credibility.

And credibility, built slowly and consistently, tends to compound more reliably than attention.

Scaling NIL: When Opportunity Grows

FILM ROOM

It started small.

A local training facility offered Asher $250 for two posts and a weekend appearance. They showed up, posted responsibly, and thanked the business. It felt manageable. Educational, even.

Three months later, two more local businesses reached out. A supplement company sent some product. A regional car dealership asked about a longer-term partnership. A sports marketing representative sent a direct message offering "brand expansion."

Nothing about this momentum was reckless. In fact, it was encouraging. But growth changes responsibility. When NIL activity moves from occasional to recurring, the conversation shifts from "Is this allowed?" to "How do we manage this well?"

Scaling NIL is not about chasing more. It is about structuring growth in a way that protects development, eligibility, academics, and emotional balance.

Growth Feels Flattering

Most high school NIL growth begins with affirmation. An athlete performs well. Visibility increases. Local businesses see value. Engagement rises. Someone says, "You're building a brand."

For a teenager, that language feels validating. For parents, it can feel like proof that the hard work is paying off.

But scaling introduces complexity in five areas that families often underestimate:

- Time management
- Academic stability
- Tax and financial structure
- Brand alignment
- Emotional identity

None of these issues are dramatic at small scale. They become meaningful as volume increases.

The Junior Who Scaled Too Fast

FILM ROOM

Ethan was a junior quarterback with moderate recruiting interest. His first NIL deal was simple: a local gym partnership tied to offseason training. It went well. Everybody was happy with the result.

Within six months, he had:

- Three local sponsorships

- A regional apparel partnership

- A weekly posting schedule

- A youth camp appearance commitment

- A new logo designed by a marketing consultant

His social media presence expanded quickly. His follower count doubled. Engagement rose. But so did the pressure.

By mid-season, Ethan was juggling:

- Practice

- Studying film

- Recruiting calls

- Homework

- Sponsored content deadlines

- Messaging brands

- Appearance scheduling

His performance dipped slightly. Nothing dramatic, but noticeable. A coach quietly asked if he was stretched too thin. Ethan insisted he could handle it, but something subtle had shifted. NIL had moved from supplemental opportunity to operational responsibility.

The issue was not money. It was management.

The First Scaling Question: Does This Still Serve Development?

Before accepting additional partnerships, families should ask a foundational question: Does this opportunity enhance or distract from athletic and academic development? Development remains the primary asset. In high school, performance growth drives recruiting value far more than brand growth does.

If NIL volume begins to:

- Reduce recovery time
- Interfere with training
- Create academic instability
- Introduce emotional stress
- Shift focus from skill development

Then scale is outpacing readiness. Growth is not always acceleration. Sometimes growth requires boundaries.

Time Becomes the Hidden Cost

Each additional deal introduces:

- Email communication
- Contract review
- Content planning
- Posting schedules
- Appearance coordination
- Reporting and deliverables

Individually, these tasks are small, but collectively, they consume hours. Parents often underestimate the administrative load. Athletes underestimate the cognitive load. One small deal feels like exposure, but five deals feel like management. When scale increases, someone must become the operational coordinator. In most high school cases, that person is a parent.

That role should be acknowledged openly.

When to Consider Formal Structure

As income increases beyond occasional payments, families should evaluate structural organization.

This is where questions about LLC formation, separate bank accounts, and accounting systems emerge. As we talked about earlier, an LLC is not automatically required for high school NIL activity.

However, it may become reasonable when:

- Multiple recurring contracts exist
- Income exceeds modest supplemental levels
- Liability concerns increase
- The athlete is entering longer-term agreements

Forming an LLC can:

- Separate personal and business finances
- Clarify income tracking
- Provide liability insulation
- Establish professional structure

It also introduces responsibilities:

- Filing requirements
- Annual reporting
- Separate tax considerations
- Possible state registration fees

Families should resist forming entities simply because it "sounds professional." Structure should follow scale, not precede it. Online formation services (such as LegalZoom or similar platforms) can handle basic entity creation, but they do not replace individualized legal advice. When income becomes meaningful or contracts complex, consultation with an attorney and CPA is prudent.

The goal is not sophistication, but clarity.

Taxes: The Conversation That Cannot Be Avoided

As NIL income increases, tax responsibility increases proportionally. High school athletes earning income are typically considered independent contractors for tax purposes. That means:

- No automatic withholding
- Self-employment tax considerations
- Quarterly estimated payments may apply
- Recordkeeping becomes essential

Parents need to understand that gross payment is not net income. If an athlete earns $10,000 in NIL income, a portion must be reserved for taxes. The exact percentage varies by state and circumstance, but failing to reserve funds creates stress later.

Scaling without tax planning creates surprise, which creates panic. Structure prevents both.

Brand Alignment Matters More at Scale

At small scale, most local deals are aligned with community familiarity. At larger scale, alignment becomes strategic.

Families should evaluate:

- Does this brand align with the athlete's values?
- Is the product appropriate for minors?
- Does the tone of the brand match the athlete's digital presence?
- Are there exclusivity clauses that limit future opportunities?

As volume increases, reputational risk increases. One poorly aligned partnership at small scale is awkward. At larger scale, it can shape perception.

Recruiting and Scaling: The Quiet Tension

Families sometimes assume more NIL visibility automatically improves recruiting prospects. This is not consistently true.

Recruiting staff evaluate:

- Performance trajectory
- Positional development
- Coachability
- Academic reliability
- Cultural fit

Large-scale NIL activity can introduce concern if it suggests distraction, over-commercialization, or misplaced focus. A modest, well-managed NIL portfolio signals maturity. An aggressive commercial identity may create skepticism.

This does not mean athletes should suppress opportunity. It means growth should appear proportional to performance.

Story: The Athlete Who Pulled Back

FILM ROOM

Sofia was a volleyball player whose sophomore year ended with a strong club season and a noticeable increase in recruiting interest. Her first NIL deal was with a local sports nutrition store. It was modest and straightforward.

Within a year, her visibility expanded. A regional apparel brand offered a partnership. A tournament director asked her to promote an upcoming event. A digital marketing consultant suggested launching branded merchandise. None of the opportunities were unreasonable. Each one made sense in isolation.

By junior spring, however, her calendar looked different than it had the year before.

Weekdays were filled with school and practice. Evenings included responding to brand emails and planning content. Weekends included tournaments, filming promotional clips, and one scheduled appearance per month.

Her parents began noticing subtle shifts. She was more irritable. Recovery time shortened. Homework felt rushed. The enthusiasm that initially surrounded NIL began to feel transactional. The breaking point was not dramatic. It was quiet. After a long tournament weekend, Sofia admitted she felt like she was "always on."

That phrase mattered.

Her parents made a decision that felt counterintuitive: they paused new deals for the remainder of the season. They fulfilled existing contracts but declined additional requests. They reduced posting frequency to focus on competition.

Recruiting interest did not disappear, in fact, performance improved slightly. Scaling down temporarily did not damage her trajectory. It stabilized it.

Growth does not have to be linear to be successful.

The Calendar Reality of Scaling

One of the most underestimated aspects of scaling NIL is calendar density. At small scale, NIL fits into free time. At larger scale, it competes with recovery and preparation. Families should think in terms of seasons.

In-Season

During the competitive season:

- Training intensity is high
- Travel increases
- Emotional volatility increases
- Academic load may peak

NIL activity during this period should be minimal and predictable. Content can be batched in advance. Appearances should be rare. New negotiations should be limited unless urgent.

The priority during season remains performance.

Offseason

Offseason windows provide better opportunities for:

- Content creation
- Appearances
- Partnership launches
- Planning sessions
- Administrative organization

Scaling is healthiest when operational tasks live primarily in offseason blocks. When NIL obligations spill heavily into postseason or playoff windows, stress compounds.

The Five Stages of NIL Scaling

Most high school athletes who scale move through predictable stages.

Stage 1: Introductory Opportunity

- One or two local deals.
- Minimal administrative burden.
- Learning phase.
- Primary focus: Education and compliance.

Stage 2: Recurring Local Partnerships

- 2–4 recurring agreements.
- Regular posting schedule.
- Some appearance obligations.
- Primary focus: Time management and basic financial tracking.

Stage 3: Regional Visibility

- Broader audience.
- Longer-term contracts.
- Possible marketing representation.
- Primary focus: Structural organization (separate accounts, accounting systems, potential entity consideration).

Stage 4: Multi-Brand Portfolio

- Several concurrent agreements.
- Increased income.
- Greater scheduling complexity.
- Primary focus: Operational discipline and brand alignment.

Stage 5: High-Exposure Scaling

- Significant income.
- Professional advisors involved.
- Long-term strategic planning.
- Primary focus: Preservation of development and long-term flexibility.

Most athletes will not move beyond Stage 2 or 3. Understanding the stages prevents premature escalation. Families sometimes attempt Stage 4 infrastructure while still in Stage 1 visibility. Structure should follow scale.

Financial Scaling

At small scale, NIL income often feels informal. An athlete earns $500 here, $750 there. Payments arrive by check or digital transfer. Taxes feel abstract. Recordkeeping is casual. As scale increases, informality becomes risk.

Let's walk through a realistic progression.

Example: Stage 2 Athlete

- 3 recurring local deals
- $600 per month average
- $7,200 annual gross income

At this level:

- Income should be tracked carefully.
- A separate bank account is advisable.
- Roughly 20–30% should be reserved for taxes (state-dependent).
- Basic spreadsheet tracking may suffice.

This is manageable. Now consider growth.

Example: Stage 3 Athlete

- 6 partnerships
- Two regional contracts
- $2,000 per month average
- $24,000 annual gross income

At this level:

- Quarterly estimated taxes may apply.
- Self-employment tax becomes meaningful.
- Accounting software becomes helpful.
- Formal bookkeeping is recommended.
- CPA consultation becomes prudent.

Now scale again.

Example: Stage 4 Athlete

- 8–10 active partnerships
- Long-term apparel agreement
- Seasonal appearance commitments
- $60,000 annual gross income

At this level:

- Entity formation (LLC) becomes reasonable.
- Written accounting procedures are necessary.
- Clear invoicing and payment tracking systems are required.
- Liability exposure should be evaluated.
- Financial planning should begin.

The key point is not the specific number. The key point is that scaling increases complexity faster than most families expect. Gross revenue is visible. Administrative responsibility is not.

Gross vs. Net: Never Too Early to Learn

When athletes begin seeing larger payment amounts, the psychological impact is real.

A $10,000 contract feels substantial.

But if:

- 25% is reserved for taxes,
- 10% goes to representation,
- 5% goes to design or marketing costs,

the net amount changes.

Understanding gross versus net income is a maturity milestone. Parents should include the athlete in these conversations as financial literacy is part of scaling responsibly.

- It prevents entitlement.
- It prevents overspending.
- It reinforces that NIL income is earned, managed, and allocated — not simply received.

Contract Evolution: How Agreements Change at Scale

Early NIL contracts are often informal and short-term. As scale increases, contract language typically becomes more structured. Families should expect:

- Longer contract durations (6–12 months rather than one-off posts)

- Exclusivity clauses within product categories
- Content quotas
- Performance metrics
- Termination conditions
- Morals clauses

Exclusivity deserves special attention. If an athlete signs a year-long apparel agreement with exclusivity in athletic wear, future opportunities with competing brands may be prohibited. Morals clauses allow brands to terminate agreements if the athlete engages in conduct deemed damaging to the brand.

At small scale, contracts may not include these clauses, but at larger scale, they almost always do.

Reading carefully becomes essential.

When To Hire an Attorney

Families sometimes hesitate to involve attorneys due to cost. Professional legal review becomes reasonable when:

- Contracts exceed modest income levels
- Exclusivity spans long durations
- Performance-based compensation is included
- Geographic rights are unclear
- Intellectual property ownership is referenced

An attorney can clarify:

- Whether NIL is properly structured
- Whether the athlete retains rights to their own content

- whether termination language is balanced
- Whether eligibility concerns are implicated

This is not overreaction; it is proportional response to scale.

Scaling Without Losing Leverage

As visibility increases, so does negotiating power, if managed well. Athletes who:

- Deliver content on time,
- Communicate professionally,
- Maintain consistent tone,
- Avoid controversy,

increase renewal probability. Renewals are often more valuable than constant new deals. Families sometimes chase expansion when stability would produce better long-term value.

Scaling responsibly means asking: Is growth coming from volume, or from strengthening existing partnerships? The latter is usually more sustainable.

Outside Representation

We touched on representation earlier, so there is no need to spend a lot of time on it in depth here, but it becomes relevant again when things start to grow. As opportunities increase, families often begin to think about bringing in outside help. In the right situation, that support can be useful. It can make negotiations smoother, provide a clearer sense of what deals are worth, help filter which brands make sense, and take some of the pressure off day-to-day coordination.

At the same time, adding representation changes the structure. It introduces commissions, longer-term agreements, and sometimes exclusivity. It can also create an expectation to keep increasing deal flow, which is not always aligned with what is best for the athlete at that stage.

Because of that, the decision deserves a careful look. If the workload is still manageable, contracts are relatively simple, and income does not yet justify giving up a percentage, it may be too early. It is also worth considering whether the athlete is ready for the added visibility and expectations that come with expanded activity.

At its best, outside help should make things easier and more organized. If it adds pressure or complexity, it is usually a sign that the timing is not quite right.

Sometimes Scaling Quietly Hurts Recruiting

Recruiting staff rarely object to reasonable NIL activity. However, scaling can raise concern if:

- Commercial messaging dominates the athlete's digital presence.
- The athlete appears distracted during evaluation windows
- Promotional commitments interfere with unofficial visits or camps.
- Public identity feels more commercial than competitive.

Coaches recruit athletes, not influencers.

An athlete whose performance growth plateaus while commercial visibility expands may invite skepticism. The solution is not secrecy, it is proportionality.

The Discipline of Margin

Margin is rarely discussed in NIL conversations. Margin means leaving space in the calendar, emotional bandwidth, academic schedule, and space for recovery.

High school athletics already demand structure. Scaling NIL without margin creates compression and that compression reduces enjoyment, which in turn affects performance.

Emotional Identity and Early Commercialization

There is also a quieter psychological shift that can happen when NIL activity expands quickly.

Teenagers are still forming identity. When attention increases, when money begins to flow, and when adults start using words like "brand" and "market positioning," it can subtly reshape how a young athlete sees themselves. That shift is not inherently negative, but it can become destabilizing if it outpaces emotional maturity.

Performance in sports is cyclical. There are strong seasons and plateau seasons. There are injuries, slumps, coaching changes, and growth phases that are not immediately visible to the outside world. If an athlete begins to anchor their identity to sponsorship momentum rather than skill development, normal performance fluctuations can feel like personal or financial failure.

Parents play a critical role here. The steady message should be that NIL is an extension of opportunity, not the foundation of identity. Training, academics, and character development remain the primary pillars. Commercial opportunity is layered on top of those foundations, not substituted for them.

Keeping that hierarchy clear prevents scaling from distorting self-perception.

Knowing When to Say No

Growth often creates a subtle pressure to accept every opportunity. Businesses express urgency. Representatives suggest momentum must be capitalized on. The athlete may feel that turning something down signals ingratitude or weakness.

In reality, selective refusal is often a sign of maturity.

Declining an opportunity because it conflicts with the competitive season, feels misaligned with personal values, or simply adds too much operational strain is not a step backward. It is an acknowledgment that development remains the priority.

Families should feel comfortable asking practical questions before accepting additional deals:

- Will this interfere with recovery or training blocks?
- Does this introduce unnecessary stress during the season?
- Is the compensation proportional to the time and responsibility involved?
- Does this contract restrict future flexibility?

Scaling responsibly includes preserving margin: time margin, emotional margin, and developmental margin.

Sustainable Growth

As NIL activity becomes more consistent, sustainability becomes the organizing principle.

That may mean limiting the number of concurrent partnerships rather than stacking them aggressively. It may mean batching content creation during offseason windows instead of scattering obligations throughout the competitive calendar. It may mean creating clear boundaries around school nights, exam periods, or playoff runs.

High school remains a developmental environment. Even for athletes with meaningful visibility, the long-term trajectory still depends far more on skill growth and academic stability than on short-term promotional volume.

When NIL integrates smoothly into that environment, it enhances opportunity. When it begins to dominate the calendar or emotional bandwidth, it quietly undermines the very foundation that created the opportunity in the first place.

Families who manage scaling well often share one common trait: they treat NIL as part of the ecosystem, not the center of it.

Integration: Growth Without Drift

When NIL activity expands, families often focus on the visible indicators of growth — income, followers, partnerships, exposure. Those metrics are easy to track. What is harder to track is drift.

Drift happens gradually. Training becomes slightly less focused. Academic effort becomes slightly more rushed. Rest becomes slightly shorter. Family conversations shift from development to deal flow. None of these changes are dramatic in isolation, but over time they accumulate.

Scaling responsibly means watching for drift. It also means periodically asking questions that have nothing to do with money:

- Is performance still improving?
- Is schoolwork stable?
- Is the athlete enjoying the sport?
- Is identity still anchored in growth rather than visibility?

If those answers remain strong, scaling is likely proportionate. If they begin to waver, the solution is rarely dramatic. It is usually structural.

High school careers are short. Long-term opportunities depend far more on skill development, maturity, and stability than on maximizing short-term sponsorship revenue.

Families who scale successfully tend to operate with quiet restraint. They recognize visibility is temporary, but development compounds. They understand opportunity expands most sustainably when it is layered onto progress rather than substituted for it.

Scaling is not about accelerating as fast as possible. It is about growing without losing direction.

Elite, Professional, and Olympic-Level High School Athletes

It does not happen often, but when it does, everything changes.

A fourteen-year-old swimmer qualifies for a national team pipeline. A gymnast earns international prize money. A soccer player signs with an MLS academy while still enrolled in high school. A baseball prospect signs internationally at sixteen. A track athlete qualifies for the Olympic Trials while still a junior.

Most families will never encounter these scenarios, but a small percentage will. And when they do, the questions are no longer about small local NIL deals or social media tone. They become structural. Legal. Eligibility-driven.

This chapter exists for the rare but real cases where high school athletics intersect with professional or semi-professional status. The stakes are higher and the margin for misunderstanding is smaller.

High School Status Does Not Automatically Equal Amateur Status

Many parents assume that if their child is enrolled in high school, they are automatically considered an amateur athlete under all governing bodies, but that is not always true.

Different organizations govern different layers:

- State high school athletic associations
- National governing bodies (USA Swimming, USA Track & Field, USA Gymnastics, etc.)
- Professional leagues (MLS, MLB international signings, overseas clubs)
- The NCAA
- International federations

An athlete can be compliant with one body and ineligible under another. This is where complexity begins.

Olympic and National Team Athletes

In sports like swimming, diving, gymnastics, track and field, wrestling, and figure skating, elite athletes often compete internationally while still in high school.

These athletes may receive:

- Prize money
- Sponsorships
- Appearance fees
- Equipment endorsements
- National team stipends

At the high school level, state associations vary widely in how they treat prize money and outside competition. Some states permit outside competition freely as long as school seasons are not violated. Others restrict compensation tied to performance during the school season. At the NCAA level, the rules are historically strict regarding:

- Accepting prize money beyond actual expenses
- Signing professional contracts
- Receiving compensation tied to athletic performance

Recent NIL changes have not erased amateurism boundaries around professional participation.

An Olympic-qualified high school athlete must evaluate:

- Is compensation tied to publicity (NIL)?
- Is it tied to performance?
- Has a professional contract been signed?
- Are agents involved?
- Does the agreement preserve collegiate eligibility?

These questions are no longer theoretical. They determine future pathways.

When the Pathway Is No Longer Linear

One of the reasons elite high school cases create confusion is most families are accustomed to a linear development model. Their child plays youth sports, improves through high school, explores recruiting conversations, and then chooses between collegiate competition or stepping away from organized athletics. Elite athletes greatly disrupt that timeline.

A swimmer may qualify for a national team event before finishing sophomore year. A gymnast may be internationally ranked at fourteen. A soccer player may be offered a homegrown contract while still enrolled in high school classes. A baseball prospect may sign internationally at sixteen.

In those moments, the athlete is no longer operating inside a single system. They operate inside overlapping systems, and each system uses different language, different eligibility definitions, and different financial rules.

Parents often expect someone to clearly explain how those systems connect. In reality, no single governing body oversees all of it. The state high school association does not manage NCAA eligibility. The NCAA does not govern professional leagues. International federations operate under yet another framework.

The family becomes the coordinating body. That responsibility requires slowing the process down, even when the opportunity feels urgent.

A Swimmer at the Crossroads

FILM ROOM

Rebecca, a junior swimmer places second at a national level meet the summer before senior year. The placement qualifies her for an international event and includes prize money. A swimwear company approaches her with an endorsement tied to her Olympic visibility. An agent offers to manage negotiations.

At the same time, several collegiate programs are recruiting her aggressively. Nothing about this scenario is improper. It is simply layered.

If she intends to compete in the NCAA, the prize money must be evaluated carefully. Historically, NCAA rules have limited prize money to actual and necessary expenses tied to competition. If the prize exceeds that amount and is retained beyond expenses, eligibility questions can arise.

The endorsement agreement must be examined for performance-based incentives. NIL compensation tied to publicity is distinct from compensation tied to athletic results. If a contract blurs that line, it can create complications later.

The agent's role must also be defined. Representation for NIL marketing purposes is treated differently from representation for professional contract negotiation. If the agent negotiates a professional contract in that sport, NCAA eligibility may be forfeited in that sport.

None of these issues are dramatic in isolation. They are technical. But technical boundaries define future options. Rebecca and her family are not deciding whether to "take the money." They are deciding which pathway they want to preserve.

Classification Matters More Than Headlines

Recent NIL reforms have led many families to believe that amateurism restrictions have largely disappeared. That perception is incomplete. While NIL allows athletes to monetize publicity rights, it does not automatically permit:

- Signing professional contracts in the same sport while preserving NCAA eligibility
- Accepting unlimited prize money beyond expenses in certain sports
- Entering into agreements that tie compensation directly to performance outcomes

The distinction between NIL and professional status remains significant.

For example, a high school soccer player training in an MLS academy environment may still be considered an amateur. The academy structure itself does not automatically eliminate eligibility. However, signing a professional contract, even at a developmental level, changes that status.

Similarly, an athlete may accept a sponsorship deal for promoting equipment or apparel. That is NIL. If the same athlete signs a contract to play professionally in that sport, the analysis changes entirely.

The classification of the agreement, not the excitement surrounding it, determines its impact.

The Decision Framework Families Need

When elite or semi-professional opportunities arise, clarity comes from structured questioning rather than emotional reaction.

First, identify the intended pathway. Is the athlete's long-term goal collegiate competition? Immediate professional participation? Olympic qualification followed by college? Or is the family open to multiple possibilities? Without defining the destination, evaluating contracts becomes reactive.

Second, determine the nature of the compensation. Is it tied to publicity, performance, or contractual participation in a professional league? Each category carries different implications.

Third, clarify representation. If an agent is involved, what exactly are they authorized to negotiate? NIL marketing representation and professional contract representation are not interchangeable. The scope of authority must be defined in writing.

Fourth, read the contract carefully. Families should review exclusivity clauses, duration, performance incentives, termination rights, and language referencing professional status. Words that seem minor can carry significant eligibility consequences.

Finally, consider the cost of patience. In many elite cases, opportunities will not disappear overnight. The fear of missing out often pressures families into fast decisions. Eligibility, however, is far more difficult to recover once surrendered.

Emotional Acceleration and Identity Shift

There is also a psychological component that deserves attention. When a fifteen-year-old begins receiving professional-level attention, expectations shift quickly. Adults may speak to the athlete differently. Media coverage may increase. Financial figures may exceed anything the family has previously managed.

High school, however, remains a developmental environment. Professional sport is performance-driven and transactional. The shift from one to the other is not only legal; it is emotional.

Parents need to ask whether the athlete is prepared for that acceleration. Are they equipped to handle scrutiny, contractual obligations, and financial responsibility? Does the structure around them include legal counsel and financial guidance?

Elite exposure magnifies strengths and vulnerabilities.

International Athletes and Prior Professional Experience

For international students enrolling in U.S. high schools, prior participation may already complicate eligibility analysis. An athlete may have competed in a professional league abroad or accepted prize money under different federation rules. When that athlete enters a U.S. high school system, disclosure becomes critical.

Eligibility bodies will often request documentation of prior contracts, compensation, and competition level. Failing to disclose information rarely resolves questions. It typically delays them. Transparency, even when uncomfortable, provides a clearer pathway forward.

When Professional Status Is Intentional

It is important to state clearly that early professional decisions are not inherently irresponsible.

In some sports — particularly those with short competitive windows — the optimal pathway may bypass collegiate athletics entirely. If an athlete is positioned for international success with significant earning potential, the professional route may be rational.

The key distinction here is intention.

Choosing professionalism knowingly, with legal guidance and financial planning, is fundamentally different from drifting into professional status through misunderstood paperwork.

A More Durable Perspective

This chapter exists for a minority of families. Most high school athletes will not face these crossroads. But for those who do, the stakes are not about a single season. They are about structural identity. Once an athlete is classified as professional in a sport, reversing that status is rarely simple.

Opportunities expand quickly at the elite level. Governance expands with them. Families who approach elite exposure with the same diligence as professional organizations tend to preserve options. Those who treat elite attention casually often discover that eligibility bodies operate with far less flexibility than media headlines suggest.

When high school and professional lines blur, caution is not strategy.

Prize Money vs. NIL vs. Professional Compensation

It helps to distinguish between three categories:

1. NIL Compensation

Payment for use of name, image, or likeness.
Example: Sponsorship post for a swim equipment brand.

2. Prize Money

Payment awarded for placement in competition.
Example: $5,000 for winning an international meet.

3. Professional Contract Compensation

Payment tied to participation in a professional league or club structure.

Each category carries different eligibility implications. High school associations often focus on whether participation undermines the educational nature of competition.

The NCAA historically focuses on whether the athlete has:

- Accepted pay for play
- Signed a professional contract
- Used an agent for professional negotiation
- Received compensation exceeding allowable limits

An athlete can earn NIL income and remain eligible. They can also earn prize money under specific limits and remain eligible. Furthermore, an athlete who signs a professional contract in certain sports may forfeit NCAA eligibility in that sport.

MLS Academies and Soccer Pathways

In soccer, particularly within Major League Soccer academies, athletes can train in professional environments while maintaining amateur eligibility.

However:

- Signing a professional contract changes status
- Receiving compensation beyond allowable development stipends may affect NCAA eligibility
- Competing in professional matches can carry implications depending on structure

Families must distinguish between:

- Academy training agreements
- Homegrown professional contracts
- NIL endorsements
- Development stipends

The terminology matters. An academy environment does not automatically equal professional status. A signed pro contract does.

International Baseball Signings

Baseball presents another unique pathway. International prospects can sign professional contracts at sixteen in certain contexts. Those athletes may still be high school–aged.

Once a professional contract is signed, NCAA baseball eligibility is typically affected.

Families must ask:

- Is the athlete choosing a professional pathway immediately?
- Or preserving the option of collegiate competition?

There is no moral judgment in either direction, but the decision is final once contractual lines are crossed.

14-Year-Olds Earning Significant Income

Rarely, an athlete in a niche or Olympic sport becomes highly marketable at a young age.

Imagine: A 14-year-old gymnast earns $150,000 in sponsorship deals tied to Olympic visibility. That income itself does not automatically create ineligibility.

But the structure matters:

- Who negotiated the deal?
- Was an agent used?
- Are there performance-based incentives?
- Are professional endorsements tied to future commitments?
- Does the contract include exclusivity clauses?

Additionally, high income introduces tax, trust, guardianship, and financial management considerations far beyond typical high school NIL situations.

At this level, families should involve:

- A qualified sports attorney
- A CPA familiar with athlete compensation
- A financial planner
- Possibly a trust or entity structure

This is no longer "local NIL," it is professional-level asset management.

Agents and Representation

The moment agents enter the conversation, clarity becomes critical. Under NCAA rules, representation for NIL purposes is permitted under certain conditions. Representation for professional contract negotiation is a different category. If an athlete signs with an agent for the purpose of securing a professional contract in a specific sport, eligibility in that sport may be compromised.

Parents must understand there is a difference between:

- NIL marketing representation
- Professional contract representation

And that difference must be documented.

International Students Competing in U.S. High Schools

Another layer emerges when international students compete in U.S. high schools.

International athletes may have:

- Previously competed professionally abroad
- Accepted prize money under different federation rules
- Signed developmental agreements overseas

When they enroll in a U.S. high school, eligibility review often includes examination of prior competition.

Families must be prepared to disclose:

- Contracts
- Prize money records
- Competition level
- Agent relationships

Transparency prevents later disqualification.

This area can become legally complex quickly.

The NCAA Intersection

Even if high school eligibility is preserved, collegiate eligibility may be affected by actions taken during high school. NCAA amateurism rules have evolved, especially after NIL changes.

However, NIL does not override:

- Professional contract prohibitions
- Pay-for-play restrictions
- Agent representation limitations
- Prize money boundaries

An athlete who intends to compete at the NCAA level must evaluate professional opportunities through that lens. Sometimes the choice is clear but other times it is a crossroads. Families should never assume high school permission equals NCAA permission. They are separate governing structures.

When Professional Is the Right Choice

It is important to say this clearly: For some athletes, turning professional while still high school–aged is the correct decision.

If:

- The athlete is a generational talent
- The financial opportunity is life-changing
- The development pathway is clear
- The family understands the long-term implications

Then professional choice is not reckless, it is strategic. But it definitely should be intentional and not accidental.

Accidental Professionalism

More common than deliberate professional signing is accidental boundary crossing.

Examples include:

- Signing an agreement without understanding exclusivity clauses
- Accepting prize money above allowable expense limits
- Allowing an agent to negotiate beyond NIL marketing
- Competing in events categorized as professional unknowingly

These mistakes are rarely malicious; they are often administrative misunderstandings. But eligibility bodies evaluate outcomes, not intentions.

- Documentation matters.
- Language matters.
- Classification matters.

The Legal Layer

When high-level compensation is involved, documentation should include:

- Clear contract language distinguishing NIL from professional play
- Defined compensation structures
- Tax withholding clarity
- Guardianship approval if under 18
- Termination clauses
- Eligibility preservation language when applicable

At this level, DIY contracts are not appropriate. This is where professional counsel protects future options.

A Measured Perspective

Most families reading this chapter will never face these decisions. This is not dismissive. It is realistic.

The overwhelming majority of high school athletes:

- Will not qualify for Olympic trials at fourteen
- Will not sign MLS professional contracts
- Will not earn six-figure endorsement deals before graduation

But a small number will. And those families need to slow down rather than speed up.

Structure Over Emotion

Across this entire book, one theme repeats: Structure protects eligibility. In edge cases, structure protects careers.

Whether the opportunity is:

- A local gym endorsement
- An international sponsorship
- An academy contract
- Prize money from world competition

The question is always the same: Is this structured in a way that preserves our intended pathway?

If the goal is to participate in collegiate athletics, decisions must align with that. If the goal is professional acceleration, the choice must be acknowledged fully. Neither path is inherently superior. But drifting into professionalism without realizing it is avoidable.

Final Perspective

Elite status does not eliminate the need for caution, it increases it. The higher the exposure, the more precise decisions must become.

Families in rare, high-level scenarios should operate with:

- Legal clarity
- Financial planning
- Transparent documentation
- Eligibility consultation
- Long-term projection

Most high school NIL decisions are about small amounts of money and local visibility. Elite edge cases are about structural identity, and that structural identity defines the rest of the career.

Multi-Sport Athletes and Late Bloomers

FILM ROOM

The phone call came during sophomore year.

Ryan's father was frustrated, not angry, just worn down. Ryan had been a three-sport athlete since middle school: football in the fall, basketball in the winter, baseball in the spring. He was competitive in all three. Not dominant, but competitive. That spring, a travel baseball coach told him something that lingered.

"If he really wants to play in college, he needs to drop the other sports. He's falling behind the kids who specialize year-round."

It wasn't said maliciously. It was framed as practical advice. Strategic. Necessary.

Ryan's parents were worried they were making a mistake by allowing him to continue playing multiple sports. They were worried that NIL opportunities, however small, would never materialize without early specialization. They were worried about visibility, recruiting momentum, and falling behind peers who seemed to have a clear lane.

Ryan, meanwhile, just liked competing.

- He liked football practice in the cold.
- He liked the rhythm of basketball season.

- He liked the long afternoons at the ballpark.

The anxiety wasn't coming from him. It was coming from the narrative surrounding him. This chapter is about that narrative.

Development timelines are not uniform. And when NIL enters the conversation, the pressure to accelerate can distort good decision-making.

The Illusion of a Single Timeline

Social media makes athletic development look linear.

- Freshman gets offer.
- Sophomore commits.
- Junior signs NIL deal.
- Senior announces early enrollment.

That sequence exists, I've even mentioned it in this book, but it is rare. Most high school athletes develop in waves, not straight lines. Growth spurts happen late, skill refinement lags and then catches up, confidence dips and rebounds, injuries interrupt momentum, and academic growth reshapes recruiting conversations.

NIL does not change biological and psychological realities. If anything, NIL has amplified the illusion that development must happen earlier.

Families see:

- Middle schoolers with highlight accounts
- Eighth graders with "brand logos"
- Sophomores announcing partnerships
- Juniors dropping merchandise

Without context, it does feel like a race.

But most recruiting decisions still hinge on upperclassman performance. Most college coaches understand that 14- and 15-year-olds are incomplete projections.

The problem is not that early visibility exists. The problem is assuming it is required.

Multi-Sport Athletes: Liability or Advantage?

There is a persistent belief that specialization is the only path to recruitment and NIL relevance. This belief is not universally supported by evidence.

Many college programs value multi-sport backgrounds because they signal:

- Diverse motor development
- Reduced overuse injury risk
- Competitive adaptability
- Mental freshness
- Broader athletic IQ

A football player who also played basketball may demonstrate lateral agility that pure year-round football players lack. A baseball player who ran track may develop explosiveness that shows up later in velocity. From a recruiting standpoint, multi-sport participation often delays peak performance but increases ceiling.

From an NIL standpoint, multi-sport athletes can actually build broader community recognition. They are visible across seasons. They interact with different peer groups. They often develop a stronger school-wide identity.

The tension arises when short-term visibility conflicts with long-term development.

Late Bloomers and the Myth of Early Offers

One of the most harmful recruiting myths is that if offers do not appear by sophomore year, the window is closing. In reality, development curves vary dramatically by sport.

In football, linemen frequently develop physically between junior and senior year. In baseball, velocity jumps often occur late in high school. In basketball, late growth spurts change positional projection entirely. Even in sports like soccer or volleyball, where club recruiting can begin early, coaches continue to evaluate upperclassman growth. NIL does not override that.

- A sophomore without an NIL deal is not behind.
- A freshman without offers is not invisible.
- A multi-sport athlete is not naïve.

They may simply be on a different clock.

The Emotional Pressure to Specialize

Parents often feel external pressure more intensely than athletes. Travel coaches imply urgency. Other parents compare timelines. Social media amplifies early success stories. When NIL enters the conversation, that urgency becomes financialized.

- "If he focuses on one sport, maybe the brand deals come sooner."
- "If she drops the others, maybe she builds a bigger following."

The problem is not ambition; it is sacrificing developmental diversity for speculative upside. If specialization improves performance naturally, that is one thing. If specialization is driven by fear, that is another. Fear is rarely a stable development strategy.

The Junior Who Was "Behind"

FILM ROOM

Elena played volleyball and ran track. She had no NIL deals and her Instagram following was modest and entirely local.

During sophomore year, several teammates began focusing exclusively on volleyball. Their club schedules intensified. Their social media presence increased. A few announced early verbal commitments.

Elena felt like she was behind, but her parents felt it more. They debated whether she should drop track to attend more offseason volleyball training events. She chose to keep both.

Junior year, she experienced a vertical jump improvement after track season. That improvement changed her blocking range. It improved her recruiting profile significantly. College coaches began calling in late junior spring — not early sophomore fall.

She never signed a major NIL deal in high school but she did sign with a Division I program. Her NIL opportunities emerged in college, when her performance stabilized at a higher level.

The early pressure to specialize might have produced incremental gains. It might also have increased burnout. Her development arc was steady. Steady wins more often than panic.

How NIL Interacts With Development Timelines

NIL opportunities are not evenly distributed across ages.

A third grader is extraordinarily unlikely to sign meaningful NIL deals. A middle schooler with a viral following is an outlier. A freshman high school athlete with substantial compensation is uncommon outside very specific circumstances.

Most high school NIL activity falls into one of three categories:

- Small local endorsements tied to community presence
- Social media partnerships based on a modest but engaged followings
- Family or business-network-driven opportunities

These do not require early specialization. In fact, athletes who diversify experiences often develop richer narratives, which later support NIL authenticity.

Brands are increasingly aware of over-manufactured youth branding. A well-rounded, grounded athlete can be more compelling than a prematurely commercialized one.

Physical Maturity vs. Skill Maturity

Another overlooked reality is biological timing. Two sophomores in the same grade may differ by 30 pounds and four inches in height. Early physical developers often dominate youth competition. Late physical developers may struggle early but surpass peers later.

Recruiting boards are filled with examples of early standouts who plateau and late bloomers who surge. NIL attention often mirrors early performance. That can distort confidence. If early physical advantage produces early visibility, families must resist confusing timing with permanence.

The athlete who peaks at 16 does not automatically peak at 21.

Micro Examples Across Sports

It helps to make this concrete, because "development curve" can feel abstract until you see it in real examples.

Football: The Late-Growing Lineman

A sophomore offensive lineman might be 6'0" and 215 pounds while a teammate is already 6'4" and 260. Recruiting attention naturally follows the larger frame early. The early developer dominates at the varsity level. But between junior and senior year, the smaller lineman grows four inches and adds 40 pounds in structured strength training. His coordination improves because he developed footwork and leverage before mass. His ceiling suddenly shifts.

College coaches who project body development are often more interested in that late-growing athlete than the early-plateau athlete. If that late developer had quit football at 14 because he was "behind," the projection would never have materialized.

Baseball: The Velocity Jump

Pitchers are famous for late velocity gains. A sophomore sitting at 82 mph is rarely recruited heavily. A senior sitting at 91 mph is recruited everywhere.

What changed?

- Sometimes it's physical maturity.

- Sometimes it's mechanical refinement.
- Sometimes it's structured strength training.

Often it's simply time.

Families who panic at 15 because radar readings lag may underestimate how much changes at 17. And NIL attention that flows to the early 88–90 mph sophomore does not guarantee long-term advantage if that athlete stalls physically. Projection matters more than early radar numbers.

Basketball: The Growth Spurt

In basketball, late growth can reshape positional identity. A sophomore point guard at 5'8" may not receive significant attention. That same athlete at 6'3" by senior year becomes a completely different prospect.

Coaches understand this. They track family height and evaluate frame. They ask about growth patterns. An athlete who plays multiple sports during that period may actually benefit from broader neuromuscular development before specializing once physical stature stabilizes.

Distance Running: The Patience Sport

In endurance sports, early success sometimes predicts stagnation later. Early maturing runners often dominate middle school competitions because of early aerobic development. Late maturers may struggle initially.

By junior or senior year, physiological ceilings shift. Athletes who develop gradually often overtake early standouts. If NIL visibility rewards the 8th-grade phenom, that does not guarantee the college scholarship conversation at 18.

Volleyball: Vertical and Strength Curve

Vertical leap and rotational power often increase significantly between sophomore and senior year with structured training. An athlete who balances volleyball and track may see measurable improvements that pure specialization does not guarantee.

The Risk of Burnout

Year-round specialization increases repetition. Repetition increases overuse injury risk. It also increases mental fatigue.

Burnout is not dramatic at first. It is subtle:

- Reduced enthusiasm
- Irritability
- Avoidance of training
- Emotional volatility
- Declining academic focus

NIL pressure layered onto specialization can accelerate that fatigue. If an athlete feels obligated to perform for followers, brands, or expectations, the psychological load increases. Development requires resilience. Resilience requires rest and perspective.

Multi-sport participation sometimes provides that balance naturally.

Recruiting Reality Check

College coaches are projecting four to five years forward.

They ask:

- What will this athlete look like at 20?
- How will they respond to adversity?
- Do they love the sport, or are they managing it?
- Are they adaptable?

A multi-sport athlete who demonstrates discipline across seasons may project stronger long-term development than a single-sport athlete who shows early saturation. NIL does not replace projection logic, it sometimes amplifies early exposure, but projection remains central.

Perspective From the Long View

Imagine two athletes:

Athlete A specializes at 13, builds a following early, signs small deals at 15, plateaus physically at 17.

Athlete B plays multiple sports, develops gradually, and enters college at 18 still improving, with a lot of room to grow.

Which timeline is more desirable? It depends on goals.

If the goal is early monetization, Athlete A appears ahead. If the goal is sustainable athletic performance at 20-22, Athlete B may hold stronger projection.

Most families reading this book are not aiming for short-term monetization at 15, they are aiming for opportunity at 18-22. That perspective changes decision-making.

The NIL Comparison Trap

Digital platforms reward early visibility, and that visibility distorts normal development curves.

You may see:

- An athlete your child used to compete with signing a partnership
- A teammate dropping a logo
- A rival posting "big announcement" graphics

Without context, it appears definitive.

But you rarely see:

- The sustainability of those deals
- The behind-the-scenes stress
- The plateau that follows
- The deals that quietly disappear

NIL announcements are public but NIL stagnation is private. Do not build your timeline around other people's highlights.

Bringing It Back to Ryan

FILM ROOM

Ryan kept playing three sports through junior year. During his Senior year, he narrowed to two. He never built a massive following. He never signed large high school NIL deals.

- He built durability.
- He avoided burnout.
- He developed physically at 17-18.
- He signed to play in college.

His timeline did not look fast, but it looked sustainable. And sustainability is undervalued in youth sports.

Development Check

Before specializing, dropping a sport, or restructuring your athlete's schedule, ask:

- Is this decision driven by evidence or comparison?
- Has my child expressed intrinsic desire to narrow focus?
- Are we responding to one person's opinion or a consistent pattern?
- Would we make the same decision if social media did not exist?
- Are we sacrificing joy for hypothetical leverage?
- Does this move improve long-term development, or just short-term visibility?

If hesitation appears in several answers, slow down. Development rarely rewards urgency.

When Different Timelines Converge

By the time athletes reach college age, something interesting happens. Early bloomers and late bloomers often converge physically.

What remains distinct is:

- Work ethic.
- Adaptability.
- Mental durability.
- Love of competition.

Multi-sport athletes frequently retain broader athletic instincts. Late bloomers often retain the hunger of competition. Early bloomers who navigated attention responsibly retain composure. In the long view, development diversity becomes an asset, not a liability. NIL opportunities in college often reflect who stabilized best, not who accelerated earliest.

Final Perspective

Multi-sport participation is not outdated.

- Late blooming is not failure.
- Delayed NIL opportunity is not missed opportunity.

Development is rarely synchronized across athletes. Families who protect long-term growth often trade short-term visibility for long-term stability.

That is not conservative, it is strategic.

If there is one principle to carry from this chapter, it is this:

Athletic development is not a race against other families. It is a progression toward your child's highest sustainable level. NIL may appear along that path but should not dictate it.

When NIL Is Not Allowed in Your State

Davaunte's parents sounded excited when they emailed the athletic director. "We just got approached by a local gym about a sponsorship," his father wrote. "It's small, just some free training and a few posts. Nothing major. NIL is allowed now, right?"

Davaunte was a junior. Solid varsity contributor. Just a good player in a competitive program. But there was one problem. In their state, high school NIL was not allowed.

Not partially restricted. Not conditionally permitted. Prohibited.

His family assumed because NIL existed nationally, because they saw headlines about college collectives and high school endorsements in other states, it applied everywhere. It did not. Fortunately, they asked before signing anything. The gym owner understood once the situation was explained. No harm done. No eligibility review. No public issue.

But it was a reminder of something important: NIL is not uniform across the country. And in some states, the answer is still no.

What "Not Allowed" Actually Means

When a state does not permit high school NIL, it typically means that student-athletes may not receive compensation for the use of their name, image, or likeness while participating in high school athletics. That prohibition usually includes:

- Paid endorsements
- Compensation for social media promotion
- Free products or services in exchange for promotion
- Paid appearances connected to athletic identity
- Booster-funded "deals"
- Advertising campaigns that rely on athletic status

In other words, if compensation is connected to an athlete's public identity as a high school athlete, and the state prohibits NIL, the activity is not permitted.

- It does not matter whether the payment is large or small.
- It does not matter whether the arrangement feels informal.
- It does not matter whether other states allow it.

Eligibility is governed locally.

Returning To "Are We Behind?"

When families learn that NIL is prohibited in their state, the reaction is often frustration.

- "Other kids are signing deals."
- "Other states are ahead."
- "Are we at a disadvantage?"

This reaction is understandable, but it is rarely accurate. The overwhelming majority of high school athletes nationwide do not earn significant NIL compensation. Even in permissive states, most high school NIL activity is modest and local.

Recruiting decisions are not contingent on whether an athlete earned money in high school. College coaches understand that NIL laws vary by state. They do not penalize athletes for living in restrictive jurisdictions. The absence of high school NIL activity does not weaken a recruiting profile.

What Is Still Allowed

Prohibition of NIL does not mean prohibition of growth. Even in restrictive states, athletes may:

- Build social media presence (without compensation)
- Create content
- Train privately
- Participate in camps and showcases
- Volunteer in the community
- Develop public speaking skills
- Prepare financially for future NIL
- Study branding and media literacy

What they may not do is monetize that presence while they remain eligible under high school rules. This distinction matters. An athlete can build discipline, reputation, and digital credibility long before monetization is permitted. Preparation is not the same as compensation.

The Temptation of Workarounds

When rules feel restrictive, creative thinking often follows. Families sometimes ask questions like:

- "What if the payment goes to a parent?"
- "What if it's just free gear?"
- "What if it's labeled as a 'gift'?"
- "What if it's a separate business arrangement?"
- "What if we wait until the season ends?"

These questions are rarely malicious. Usually, they are attempts to reconcile opportunity with restriction. But high school associations generally evaluate substance over form.

If compensation is connected to athletic identity, and the state prohibits NIL, restructuring the payment vehicle does not eliminate risk. Routing payment through a parent does not change the underlying purpose. Nor does calling compensation a "gift" automatically neutralize it.

Deleting posts does not erase documentation.

Eligibility reviews are rarely impressed by technicalities. This is where families must resist the urge to get clever. Compliance is rarely harmed by caution, but eligibility can be harmed by improvisation.

Influencer Activity: Where the Line Actually Sits

This is the area that requires the most nuance.

- What if an athlete builds a following unrelated to sports?
- What if they create content about fashion, music, cooking, gaming, or travel?

If the content is genuinely unrelated to athletic identity, and compensation is not tied to status as a high school athlete, it may fall outside athletic association jurisdiction.

However, if the athlete's following exists primarily because of athletic participation, and brands approach them because of that identity, the connection becomes harder to separate.

The safest approach in restrictive states is to assume that monetization connected to public visibility during athletic eligibility carries risk.

If families believe an arrangement falls outside athletic NIL, they should consult:

- The state athletic association
- The school's athletic director
- Qualified legal counsel familiar with state rules

Guessing is not a good strategy.

The Risk of Quiet Violations

Some families assume that small, local arrangements are unlikely to be noticed. But enforcement is often reactive.

Most high school eligibility reviews begin when:

- Another parent raises a concern
- A rival program files a complaint
- A social media post circulates
- A booster conversation surfaces
- A coach becomes aware of compensation

Small arrangements are not immune from visibility. In fact, small communities sometimes increase visibility. The reputational cost of a minor violation often outweighs the financial benefit of the arrangement.

High school careers are short.

Recruiting Without High School NIL

Even in permissive states, many families choose not to pursue high school NIL because the financial upside is limited and the compliance burden is significant.

College recruiting staff focus on:

- Film
- Measurables
- Performance trends
- Academic profile
- Character references
- Injury history
- Coachability

They are not asking, "How much NIL money did this athlete earn at 16?" They are projecting development. If an athlete in a restrictive state performs at a high level, recruiting interest follows. If an athlete in a permissive state performs at a high level, recruiting interest follows. The state NIL framework does not determine athletic ceiling.

A Different Perspective: The Advantage of Delay

There is another way to view restrictive states. Delay can create discipline. Athletes who cannot monetize early are sometimes spared the distraction of early commercialization.

They focus on:

- Skill refinement
- Physical development
- Academic stability
- Team culture

Build credibility before compensation enters the equation. Early monetization is not automatically harmful, but delayed monetization is not automatically harmful either. For many families, it simplifies the high school years.

Preparing for College NIL Without Violating High School Rules

Even in restrictive states, families can prepare responsibly. This preparation might include:

- Learning how contracts work conceptually
- Understanding basic tax principles
- Studying brand alignment
- Practicing professional email communication
- Building digital discipline
- Keeping organized performance data
- Developing public speaking skills

These actions do not involve compensation, they involve education. When athletes arrive at college, they will not start from zero.

The Psychological Reset

When NIL is not allowed, families often need to recalibrate expectations. Instead of asking, "How do we monetize this year?" the better question becomes: "How do we maximize development this year?"

Instead of asking, "Are we missing out?" the question becomes: "Are we building a stronger foundation?"

High school athletics were structured long before NIL existed. Scholarships were awarded long before NIL existed. NIL is an addition to the ecosystem, but it is not the ecosystem.

A Practical Checklist for Restrictive States

If you live in a state where NIL is prohibited:

- Confirm the rule directly from the state athletic association website.
- Review any district-level guidance.
- Inform potential sponsors politely that compensation is not permitted under current rules.
- Avoid informal or undocumented arrangements.
- Keep your focus on performance and academics.
- Revisit NIL possibilities if the law changes.

Many states have adjusted their policies over time. Monitoring updates annually is sufficient.

If the Law Changes

NIL frameworks are ever evolving. If your state shifts from prohibition to permissive policy, the transition usually includes:

- Implementation guidance
- Disclosure requirements
- School-level procedures
- Association clarifications

When that happens, approach the new opportunity slowly. The fact that something becomes permitted does not mean it becomes urgent.

Final Perspective

When NIL is not allowed in your state, the path forward is clear.

- They develop.
- They compete.
- They build character.
- They prepare.
- They do not monetize — yet. That "yet" matters.

High school eligibility is temporary while athletic development is cumulative.

Families who treat restrictive environments as developmental incubators rather than missed opportunities often discover that nothing essential was lost. NIL may enter the picture later.

What matters most is whether the athlete is ready, physically, mentally, and professionally, when it does.

Glossary of NIL and Recruiting Terms

The world of recruiting and NIL includes terminology that may be unfamiliar to many families. The following glossary explains commonly used terms in plain language to help parents and athletes better understand how opportunities, rules, and agreements work in practice.

Agent — A professional representative who helps athletes negotiate endorsement deals, sponsorships, or professional contracts. At the high school level, the use of agents may be restricted by athletic associations and should be reviewed carefully before entering any agreement.

Amateur Status — The eligibility classification that allows an athlete to participate in school or collegiate athletics. Receiving certain types of compensation tied to athletic performance can jeopardize amateur status under some governing rules.

Appearance Fee — Payment provided to an athlete for attending a promotional event, clinic, signing, or community appearance as part of an NIL agreement.

Athletic Director (AD) — A school administrator responsible for managing athletic programs, enforcing eligibility rules, and overseeing compliance with state athletic association policies.

Booster — An individual or organization that provides financial or material support to a school's athletic program. Booster involvement in NIL arrangements can raise concerns if compensation appears tied to team participation or recruiting.

Brand Partnership — A promotional agreement between an athlete and a business in which the athlete promotes a company's product, service, or brand in exchange for compensation or other benefits.

Branding — The way an athlete presents their identity publicly through social media, community reputation, and personal image.

Business Entity — A legal structure used to conduct business activities. Examples include sole proprietorships, partnerships, and limited liability companies (LLCs). Some athletes use a business entity to organize NIL income or agreements.

Camp — A sports training event where athletes receive instruction, skill development, and competition opportunities. Camps are usually organized by schools, coaches, or private training organizations and typically involve multiple athletes participating together. Camps are primarily instructional rather than promotional activities.

Clinic — A shorter instructional event focused on teaching specific skills or techniques. Clinics are often conducted by coaches, trainers, or experienced athletes. In some NIL situations, athletes may be compensated for assisting with or appearing at a clinic if the activity complies with school and athletic association rules.

Collective — An organization, usually associated with college athletics, that pools financial resources to create NIL opportunities for athletes. Collectives are primarily relevant at the college level.

Compliance — The process of following rules established by athletic associations, schools, and applicable laws.

Compensation — Payment or benefits received in exchange for services or promotional activity. In NIL agreements, compensation may include money, free products, services, or discounts. Compensation must be tied to legitimate promotional activity and cannot be based on athletic performance, playing time, or team success.

Contact Period — A recruiting window defined by the NCAA during which college coaches may have direct communication with prospective student-athletes and their families.

Content Creation — The process of producing digital material such as photos, videos, or posts used for social media or promotional activity.

Contract — A written agreement outlining the terms of an NIL partnership, including responsibilities, compensation, and expectations.

Deductible Expense — A business-related cost that may reduce taxable income. In NIL situations, certain expenses such as equipment used for promotional work or travel for appearances may qualify as deductible expenses.

Deliverables — The specific actions an athlete agrees to complete in an NIL agreement, such as social media posts, appearances, or promotional content.

Digital Footprint — The collection of an individual's online activity, including posts, images, comments, and videos that remain accessible over time.

Disclosure — The act of informing a school or athletic association about an NIL agreement or activity when required by policy.

Eligibility — The status that determines whether a student-athlete is allowed to compete in school athletics under governing rules.

Endorsement — A promotional agreement in which an athlete publicly supports or advertises a product, service, or brand.

Estimated Taxes — Periodic tax payments made to the government throughout the year by individuals who earn income that is not subject to automatic withholding.

Evaluation Period — A recruiting period during which college coaches may observe athletes compete but may have limited direct communication with them.

Exclusivity Clause — A provision in a contract that prevents an athlete from promoting competing businesses during the term of an agreement.

Fair Market Value — The reasonable value of services provided in an NIL agreement. Compensation should reflect the promotional work performed rather than functioning as disguised pay-for-play.

Gross Income — The total amount of money earned before taxes or expenses are deducted.

High School Athletic Association — The governing organization responsible for overseeing interscholastic athletics within a state.

Image Rights — The legal right to control how one's likeness or appearance is used in advertising or promotional materials.

Improper Benefit — A benefit provided to an athlete that violates eligibility rules. Improper benefits may include compensation tied to performance or recruiting influence.

Independent Contractor — A person who earns income for services performed but is not considered an employee of the company paying them. Most NIL compensation treats athletes as independent contractors.

Inducement — A benefit offered to influence a student-athlete's decision to enroll at, remain at, or transfer to a particular school.

Influencer — A person who promotes products or services through social media to an audience of followers.

Institutional Control — The responsibility of schools and athletic programs to monitor and enforce compliance with athletic association rules.

Limited Liability Company (LLC) — A legal business structure used to manage income, contracts, and liability related to business activities. Some athletes create an LLC to organize NIL income or partnerships. For most high school NIL activity, forming an LLC is not required.

Local Market Value — The realistic promotional value an athlete has within their community.

Marketing Rights — Permissions granted to a business allowing them to use an athlete's name, image, or likeness in advertising or promotions.

Monetization — The process of earning revenue through online content, promotional activity, or brand partnerships.

Name, Image, and Likeness (NIL) — The legal right of individuals to control and profit from the commercial use of their name, image, or personal identity.

NIL Agreement — A formal or informal arrangement in which an athlete receives compensation in exchange for promotional activity using their name, image, or likeness.

NIL Disclosure Form — A document required by some schools or associations to record NIL activity for compliance purposes.

NIL Marketplace — A platform that connects athletes with businesses seeking promotional partnerships.

Net Income — Income remaining after allowable expenses have been deducted from gross income.

Pay-for-Performance — A form of compensation tied directly to athletic outcomes such as wins, statistics, playing time, or team success. This type of arrangement is prohibited in high school athletics.

Pay-for-Play — Compensation provided directly for athletic performance, playing time, or team success. Pay-for-play is prohibited in high school athletics.

Personal Brand — The public identity and reputation an athlete develops through performance, behavior, and online presence.

Promotional Appearance — An event where an athlete attends or participates as part of an NIL agreement with a business or organization.

Promotional Activity — Work performed by an athlete as part of an NIL agreement, such as social media posts, advertising appearances, public events, or youth clinics.

Publicity Rights — Legal protections allowing individuals to control how their identity is used commercially.

Recruiting — The process by which college athletic programs identify and evaluate prospective student-athletes.

Recruiting Board — An internal list maintained by college programs ranking potential recruits.

Recruiting Inducement — An offer of benefits intended to influence an athlete's recruiting decision or school choice.

Representation — Professional assistance provided by an agent, attorney, or advisor to help manage NIL opportunities.

Roster Spot — An available position on a college team that a coach may offer to a recruit.

School Policy — Rules established by a school district or athletic department governing student conduct and NIL participation.

Self-Employment Tax — A tax applied to income earned as an independent contractor that covers Social Security and Medicare contributions.

Signing Day — The official date when athletes sign a National Letter of Intent committing to a college athletic program.

Social Media Presence — The way athletes present themselves online through platforms such as Instagram, TikTok, or YouTube.

Sole Proprietorship — The simplest business structure in which an individual earns income directly without forming a separate legal entity. Many athletes receiving NIL income operate as sole proprietors.

Sponsor — A business that compensates an athlete in exchange for promotional exposure.

Student-Athlete — A student who participates in school-sponsored athletic programs.

Tax Liability — The total amount of taxes owed to the government based on income earned during a tax year.

Term Length — The period of time an NIL agreement remains active. Termination Clause — A section of a contract describing how either party may end the agreement early.

Third-Party Representative — An individual who assists athletes with NIL opportunities, such as an agent, attorney, or marketing consultant.

Transfer Rules — Policies governing when and how a student-athlete may change schools while maintaining athletic eligibility.

Unofficial Visit — A college campus visit paid for by the athlete or their family rather than the university.

Usage Rights — Permissions granted to a business allowing them to use an athlete's name, image, or likeness in advertising or promotional materials.

Visibility — The amount of public attention an athlete receives through performance or media exposure.

Walk-On — An athlete who joins a college team without an athletic scholarship.

W-9 Form — A tax form used to provide a taxpayer identification number to a business. Athletes may complete a W-9 before receiving NIL payments.

1099-NEC (Form 1099-NEC) — A tax form used to report income earned as a non-employee. Businesses that pay an athlete $600 or more for NIL services may issue this form.

Write-Off — An informal term referring to a deductible expense that reduces taxable income.

How to Read Your State's NIL Rules

FILM ROOM

The email subject line read: "URGENT – NIL Violation Notice." It wasn't actually urgent, but it felt that way.

Kevin, a parent in a neighboring state, had printed a blog post summarizing high school NIL rules and assumed it applied locally. The article was accurate — for that state. But he never verified whether their own state's athletic association had adopted similar language.

Instead, he relied on secondary commentary. Their state had one additional disclosure requirement that the blog post did not mention. It wasn't malicious. It wasn't secretive. It simply wasn't widely advertised. They just missed it. The violation was minor. The fix was simple. But the stress was unnecessary.

This chapter exists for one reason: So you never have to rely on someone else's interpretation when you can read the rule yourself. You do not need to be a lawyer to understand your state's NIL structure, you need a framework.

The Problem With Summaries

Most families encounter state NIL information through:

- Social media posts
- Blog summaries
- Recruiting forums
- Word-of-mouth
- Outdated articles
- National-level commentary

Those sources are often well-intentioned. But they carry risks:

- They may be outdated.
- They may summarize incorrectly.
- They may omit local district overlays.
- They may apply to a different state entirely.
- They may reflect proposed rules, not adopted ones.

High school NIL is not the same nationwide.

Even states that appear similar may differ in:

- Disclosure requirements
- Logo restrictions
- Transfer limitations
- Timing rules
- Booster involvement boundaries
- Association enforcement authority

If you rely solely on commentary, you inherit someone else's assumptions. Reading the rule yourself removes that layer.

The Four-Document Rule

In most states, NIL governance at the high school level lives across four places:

- State statute (if enacted)
- State high school athletic association policy
- School district policy
- Athletic handbook or administrative procedure

Many families only read one, that's where confusion begins.

Start With the Association

Even if state law permits NIL, the athletic association often provides:

- Implementation guidance
- Example forms
- Definitions
- Eligibility clarifications
- Prohibited categories (gambling, alcohol, etc.)

Search for: "[Your State] high school NIL policy site:.org"

Avoid relying on secondary blogs. Download the PDF, save it, and read it slowly. You are not looking for legal language mastery; you are looking for structure.

What to Look For First

When opening a state NIL document, don't start by reading line-by-line. Scan for these key headings:

- Definitions
- Compensation limitations
- Disclosure requirements
- Prohibited conduct
- Use of school marks
- Third-party involvement
- Enforcement mechanisms
- Transfer or inducement language

These sections tell you where risk lives. If a rule document is ten pages long, most meaningful compliance language usually sits in 2–3 pages. Your job is to find those pages.

Understanding Definitions

Definitions matter more than most parents realize.
For example, how does your state define:

- "Compensation"
- "Endorsement"
- "Pay-for-play"
- "Booster"
- "Recruiting inducement"
- "School marks"

Small differences in wording can change interpretation. If "compensation" includes non-cash benefits, that affects free products. If "booster" includes "any individual who supports an athletic program," that widens exposure. If "school marks" include colors and mascots, not just logos, that affects apparel usage.

Never assume definitions match what you see on television at the college level.

State Law vs. Association Policy

In some states, NIL begins with legislation. In others, it begins with association vote.

If legislation exists, it may:

- Grant permission
- Limit association restrictions
- Define athlete rights

But legislation often lacks operational detail. That's where Associations fill in the implementation details.

This means: Even if the statute sounds permissive, association guidance may still regulate structure. State law may say, "Athletes may earn compensation." But the association policy may say, "Disclosure must occur within X days and no school marks may be used."

Both apply.

District Policy

Once you understand state-level rules, move to district level.

Search: "[Your District Name] NIL policy"

You may find:

- Board policy language
- Superintendent guidance
- Athletic department procedures
- Required disclosure forms

Districts sometimes add:

- Pre-approval requirements
- Form submission deadlines
- Specific contract language expectations
- Communication requirements with coaches

State permission does not eliminate district processes. Most eligibility issues arise here, not at the state level.

How to Read Prohibited Conduct Sections

Every NIL policy contains prohibitions. It is important to read this section carefully.

Look for restrictions related to:

- Gambling
- Alcohol
- Tobacco

- Adult entertainment
- Controlled substances
- Political endorsements
- School uniform usage
- Facility usage
- Performance-based compensation
- Inducements tied to enrollment

Do not skim this section. It is vitally important.

Prohibited sections often contain phrases like:

- "Directly or indirectly tied to…"
- "Contingent upon…"
- "Connected to participation…"
- "Related to enrollment…"

Those phrases matter, they reveal how broadly the rule applies.

Transfer Language: The Subtle Section

If your athlete is considering transferring schools, read the transfer section with particular care. Even if NIL is permitted, inducement language often intersects with transfer rules.

Look for:

- Benefits offered prior to enrollment
- Compensation contingent on remaining enrolled
- Third-party involvement in enrollment decisions

If NIL discussions precede a transfer, documentation, timing, and intent matter. The language signals how your state interprets these situations.

Disclosure: Timing and Method

Disclosure requirements vary widely. Some states require:

- Disclosure within a specific number of days
- Submission of contracts
- Standardized reporting forms
- Notification before execution
- Notification after execution

These differences are critical. "Within 7 days" is different than "prior approval required." If timing language is unclear, contact the athletic director and ask for written clarification. Document the answer.

What If Your State Has No Clear Policy?

Some states are still evolving. If your association website lacks clear NIL guidance:

- Check recent board meeting minutes.
- Search for press releases.
- Contact the association directly.

Ask your athletic director what current practice is.

Absence of clarity does not equal absence of rules. It means implementation may be handled case-by-case. When policy is evolving, documentation becomes even more important.

How to Evaluate Updates

NIL regulations change frequently. Before each school year:

- Revisit association website.
- Confirm there were no amendments.
- Check for FAQ updates.
- Review district handbook revisions.

Do not assume last year's rule remains unchanged. A 10-minute annual review prevents surprises.

A Review Framework

Here is a simple structure to follow whenever reviewing NIL rules:

- What is clearly allowed?
- What is clearly prohibited?
- What requires disclosure?
- What requires prior approval?
- What language references enrollment or transfers?
- What references boosters?
- What references school branding?
- What enforcement authority is described?

If you can answer those eight questions, you understand your state's NIL framework.

When to Seek Clarification

If rule language includes phrases like:

- "Subject to interpretation"
- "At the discretion of…"
- "Reasonable compensation"
- "May constitute…"

Those are gray areas. Gray areas are not violations, they are signals to communicate.

Email the athletic director: "We reviewed the association's NIL guidance and want to ensure we interpret this section correctly…"

Clarity early prevents friction later.

A Word About Third-Party Platforms

Some states reference approved third-party NIL platforms. Others prohibit school involvement in facilitating deals.

Read carefully whether:

- Schools may assist in connecting athletes with businesses.
- Coaches may share NIL opportunities.
- Third-party agents must be registered.
- Contracts must be reviewed by specific entities.

Do not assume college-level collective models apply. High school governance is often more restrictive.

Rules Are There To Help

Rules exist not to eliminate opportunity but to maintain:

- Competitive equity
- Educational focus
- Enrollment integrity
- Program stability

When parents read rules directly rather than relying on commentary, fear decreases and confidence increases.

Final Perspective

You do not need to memorize your state's NIL policy, but:

- You need to understand it.
- You need to know where it lives.
- You need to review it annually.
- You need to read definitions carefully.
- You need to respect disclosure timing.

And when in doubt, you need to ask.

That is not overcautious, it is responsible.

NIL is a privilege layered onto educational athletics. Families who understand their state's structure move calmly.

State-by-State NIL Guidelines

One of the most confusing aspects of Name, Image, and Likeness at the high school level is that there is no single national rulebook. Unlike college athletics, which are largely governed by the NCAA, high school sports are regulated at both the state and local level. Each state has its own athletic association, and many school districts also establish their own policies regarding NIL activity. As a result, the rules that apply to a student-athlete in one state may look very different from the rules that apply in another.

Some states allow high school athletes to participate in NIL activities with relatively few restrictions. Others allow NIL but require disclosure to schools or athletic associations. A small number of states still prohibit NIL activity at the high school level entirely.

Because of this variation, families often struggle to find clear information. Many parents begin their search by asking a simple question: "Is NIL allowed in our state?" The answer is rarely just yes or no. In most cases, it depends on a combination of state athletic association rules, local school policies, and how those policies are interpreted by school administrators.

This section is designed to provide a quick reference overview of NIL policies across all fifty states. Each entry identifies the general status of high school NIL activity and highlights several common compliance questions families often ask.

These summaries are not intended to replace official guidance from your state athletic association or school district. Policies change, interpretations evolve, and schools may adopt additional procedures that are not reflected in statewide rules. Families should always verify current requirements directly with their school's athletic department or governing association before participating in NIL activities.

The goal of this section is not to provide legal advice, but to help families ask better questions and understand the general landscape.

Common NIL Restrictions Across Many States

While NIL rules vary significantly from state to state, many high school athletic associations place similar limits on the types of endorsements student-athletes may participate in. These restrictions are generally intended to protect student-athletes and maintain the educational purpose of school athletics.

Although the exact language differs, the following categories are commonly restricted or prohibited in high school NIL policies:

- Alcohol or alcoholic beverage promotion
- Tobacco, nicotine, or vaping products
- Gambling or sports betting platforms
- Adult entertainment businesses
- Cannabis or marijuana products
- Illegal drugs or controlled substances
- Certain weapons or firearms promotions
- Businesses intended primarily for adult audiences

In addition, many states prohibit NIL agreements that:

- Compensate athletes for athletic performance
- Influence a student's decision to enroll at a particular school
- Involve coaches or school staff arranging deals
- Use school logos, uniforms, or facilities without permission

Even when NIL activity is allowed, most states maintain strict rules against pay-for-play arrangements or recruiting inducements.

How to Use the State Listings

Each state in the following section provides a simplified overview of several common NIL policy questions, such as whether NIL activity is permitted, whether disclosure may be required, and which organizations oversee high school athletics in that state.

When reviewing your state's entry, it may also be helpful to remember the layered structure discussed earlier in this book: State law may establish general NIL permission, state athletic associations set eligibility rules, and local school districts may adopt additional procedures or restrictions.

Understanding how those layers interact can help families avoid confusion and approach NIL opportunities more thoughtfully.

You can use the following listings as a quick reference for your state. The entries are organized alphabetically to make it easier to locate your state and review the general NIL structure that applies to high school athletes there. As you read, remember that local school policies and athletic association interpretations may influence how these rules are applied in practice. When in doubt, your school's athletic director and your state athletic association remain the most reliable sources for current guidance.

While every effort has been made to provide accurate and current information, policies regarding Name, Image, and Likeness (NIL), athletic eligibility, and school regulations may change. Readers should consult their state athletic association, school administrators, or qualified professionals for current guidance related to their specific situation.

State NIL Guidelines

ALABAMA
State Athletic Association: Alabama High School Athletic Association
Association Website: https://www.ahsaa.com/
High School NIL Allowed: No
Disclosure Required: N/A
Prior Approval Required: N/A
School Logo Use: N/A
Booster Involvement Prohibited: N/A
Governance: Athletic Association
Transfer Inducement Language: N/A
Prohibited Categories: N/A
Policy Updated: February 3, 2022

NOTES: Alabama once allowed NIL, but it was repealed in 2022.

ALASKA
State Athletic Association: Alaska School Activities Association
Association Website: https://asaa.org/
High School NIL Allowed: Yes
Disclosure Required: Unclear
Prior Approval Required: Unclear
School Logo Use: Prohibited
Booster Involvement Prohibited: Unclear
Governance: Athletic Association
Transfer Inducement Language: Yes
Prohibited Categories: Yes
Policy Updated: N/A

ARIZONA

State Athletic Association: Arizona Interscholastic Association
Association Website: https://aiaonline.org/
High School NIL Allowed: Yes
Disclosure Required: Unclear
Prior Approval Required: Unclear
School Logo Use: Prohibited
Booster Involvement Prohibited: Yes
Governance: Legislation and Athletic Association
Transfer Inducement Language: Yes
Prohibited Categories: Yes
Policy Updated: July 23, 2021

ARKANSAS

State Athletic Association: Arkansas Activities Association
Association Website: https://www.ahsaa.org/
High School NIL Allowed: Limited
Disclosure Required: Yes
Prior Approval Required: Unclear
School Logo Use: Prohibited
Booster Involvement Prohibited: Yes
Governance: Legislation
Transfer Inducement Language: Yes
Prohibited Categories: Yes
Policy Updated: April 2023
NOTES: Only committed athletes can participate

CALIFORNIA

State Athletic Association: California Interscholastic Federation

Association Website: https://www.cifstate.org/landing/index

High School NIL Allowed: Yes

Disclosure Required: Varies

Prior Approval Required: Unclear

School Logo Use: Prohibited

Booster Involvement Prohibited: Yes

Governance: Legislation and Athletic Association

Transfer Inducement Language: Yes

Prohibited Categories: Yes

Policy Updated: September 30, 2019

COLORADO

State Athletic Association: Colorado High School Activities Association

Association Website: https://chsaanow.com/

High School NIL Allowed: Yes

Disclosure Required: Yes

Prior Approval Required: Yes

School Logo Use: Prohibited

Booster Involvement Prohibited: Yes

Governance: Legislation and Athletic Association

Transfer Inducement Language: Yes

Prohibited Categories: Yes

Policy Updated: March 2020

CONNECTICUT

State Athletic Association: Connecticut Interscholastic Athletic Conference
Association Website: https://www.casciac.org/
High School NIL Allowed: Yes
Disclosure Required: Yes
Prior Approval Required: Yes
School Logo Use: Prohibited
Booster Involvement Prohibited: Yes
Governance: Legislation and Athletic Association
Transfer Inducement Language: Yes
Prohibited Categories: Yes
Policy Updated: June 2021

DELAWARE

State Athletic Association: Delaware Interscholastic Athletic Association
Association Website: https://education.delaware.gov/diaa/
High School NIL Allowed: Yes
Disclosure Required: Yes
Prior Approval Required: No
School Logo Use: Prohibited
Booster Involvement Prohibited: Yes
Governance: Legislation
Transfer Inducement Language: Yes
Prohibited Categories: Yes
Policy Updated: August 2021

FLORIDA

State Athletic Association: Florida High School Athletic Association
Association Website: https://fhsaa.com/index.aspx
High School NIL Allowed: Yes
Disclosure Required: Yes
Prior Approval Required: No
School Logo Use: Prohibited
Booster Involvement Prohibited: Yes
Governance: Legislation and Athletic Association
Transfer Inducement Language: Yes
Prohibited Categories: Yes
Policy Updated: July 2025

GEORGIA

State Athletic Association: Georgia High School Association
Association Website: https://www.ghsa.net/
High School NIL Allowed: Yes
Disclosure Required: Yes
Prior Approval Required: No
School Logo Use: Prohibited
Booster Involvement Prohibited: Yes
Governance: Legislation and Athletic Association
Transfer Inducement Language: Yes
Prohibited Categories: Yes
Policy Updated: May 2021

HAWAII
State Athletic Association: Hawaii High School Athletic Association
Association Website: https://hhsaa.org/
High School NIL Allowed: No
Disclosure Required: N/A
Prior Approval Required: Unclear
School Logo Use: N/A
Booster Involvement Prohibited: N/A
Governance: Athletic Association
Transfer Inducement Language: N/A
Prohibited Categories: N/A
Policy Updated: N/A

IDAHO
State Athletic Association: Idaho High School Activities Association
Association Website: https://idhsaa.org/
High School NIL Allowed: Yes
Disclosure Required: Yes
Prior Approval Required: No
School Logo Use: Prohibited
Booster Involvement Prohibited: Yes
Governance: Athletic Association
Transfer Inducement Language: Yes
Prohibited Categories: Yes
Policy Updated: N/A

ILLINOIS

State Athletic Association: Illinois High School Association
Association Website: https://www.ihsa.org/
High School NIL Allowed: Yes
Disclosure Required: Yes
Prior Approval Required: No
School Logo Use: Prohibited
Booster Involvement Prohibited: Yes
Governance: Legislation
Transfer Inducement Language: Yes
Prohibited Categories: Yes
Policy Updated: June 2021

INDIANA

State Athletic Association: Indiana High School Athletic Association
Association Website: https://www.ihsaa.org/
High School NIL Allowed: No
Disclosure Required: N/A
Prior Approval Required: Unclear
School Logo Use: N/A
Booster Involvement Prohibited: N/A
Governance: Athletic Association
Transfer Inducement Language: N/A
Prohibited Categories: N/A
Policy Updated: N/A

IOWA

State Athletic Association: Iowa High School Athletic Association (Boys)

Association Website: https://www.iahsaa.org (Boys)

Iowa Girls High School Athletic Union (Girls)

Association Website: https://ighsau.org (Girls)

High School NIL Allowed: Yes

Disclosure Required: Yes

Prior Approval Required: No

School Logo Use: Prohibited

Booster Involvement Prohibited: Yes

Governance: Athletic Association

Transfer Inducement Language: Yes

Prohibited Categories: Yes

Policy Updated: N/A

KANSAS

State Athletic Association: Kansas State High School Activities Association

Association Website: https://www.kshsaa.org/

High School NIL Allowed: Yes

Disclosure Required: Yes

Prior Approval Required: No

School Logo Use: Prohibited

Booster Involvement Prohibited: Yes

Governance: Athletic Association

Transfer Inducement Language: Yes

Prohibited Categories: Yes

Policy Updated: N/A

KENTUCKY

State Athletic Association: Kentucky High School Athletic Association
Association Website: https://khsaa.org/
High School NIL Allowed: Yes
Disclosure Required: Yes
Prior Approval Required: No
School Logo Use: Prohibited
Booster Involvement Prohibited: Yes
Governance: Legislation
Transfer Inducement Language: Yes
Prohibited Categories: Yes
Policy Updated: March 2022

LOUISIANA

State Athletic Association: Louisiana High School Athletic Association
Association Website: https://www.lhsaa.org/
High School NIL Allowed: Yes
Disclosure Required: Yes
Prior Approval Required: No
School Logo Use: Prohibited
Booster Involvement Prohibited: Yes
Governance: Legislation and Athletic Association
Transfer Inducement Language: Yes
Prohibited Categories: Yes
Policy Updated: June 2021

MAINE

State Athletic Association: Maine Principals' Association
Association Website: https://www.mpa.cc/
High School NIL Allowed: Yes
Disclosure Required: Yes
Prior Approval Required: No
School Logo Use: Prohibited
Booster Involvement Prohibited: Yes
Governance: Legislation
Transfer Inducement Language: Yes
Prohibited Categories: Yes
Policy Updated: June 2021

MARYLAND

State Athletic Association: Maryland Public Secondary Schools Athletic
Association
Association Website: https://www.mpssaa.org/
High School NIL Allowed: Yes
Disclosure Required: Yes
Prior Approval Required: No
School Logo Use: Prohibited
Booster Involvement Prohibited: Yes
Governance: Legislation
Transfer Inducement Language: Yes
Prohibited Categories: Yes
Policy Updated: May 2022

MASSACHUSETTS

State Athletic Association: Massachusetts Interscholastic Athletic Association

Association Website: https://www.miaa.net/

High School NIL Allowed: Yes

Disclosure Required: Yes

Prior Approval Required: No

School Logo Use: Prohibited

Booster Involvement Prohibited: Yes

Governance: Athletic Association

Transfer Inducement Language: Yes

Prohibited Categories: Yes

Policy Updated: N/A

MICHIGAN

State Athletic Association: Michigan High School Athletic Association

Association Website: https://www.mhsaa.com/

High School NIL Allowed: Yes

Disclosure Required: Yes

Prior Approval Required: Yes

School Logo Use: Prohibited

Booster Involvement Prohibited: Yes

Governance: Legislation and Athletic Association

Transfer Inducement Language: Yes

Prohibited Categories: Yes

Policy Updated: December 2020

MINNESOTA

State Athletic Association: Minnesota State High School League
Association Website: https://www.mshsl.org/
High School NIL Allowed: Yes
Disclosure Required: Yes
Prior Approval Required: No
School Logo Use: Prohibited
Booster Involvement Prohibited: Yes
Governance: Athletic Association
Transfer Inducement Language: Yes
Prohibited Categories: Yes
Policy Updated: N/A

MISSISSIPPI

State Athletic Association: Mississippi High School Activities Association
Association Website: https://www.misshsaa.com/
High School NIL Allowed: No
Disclosure Required: N/A
Prior Approval Required: N/A
School Logo Use: N/A
Booster Involvement Prohibited: N/A
Governance: Legislation
Transfer Inducement Language: N/A
Prohibited Categories: N/A
Policy Updated: April 2021

MISSOURI

State Athletic Association: Missouri State High School Activities Association

Association Website: https://www.mshsaa.org/

High School NIL Allowed: Yes

Disclosure Required: Yes

Prior Approval Required: Yes

School Logo Use: Prohibited

Booster Involvement Prohibited: Yes

Governance: Legislation

Transfer Inducement Language: Yes

Prohibited Categories: Yes

Policy Updated: July 2023

MONTANA

State Athletic Association: Montana High School Association

Association Website: https://www.mhsa.org/

High School NIL Allowed: No

Disclosure Required: N/A

Prior Approval Required: N/A

School Logo Use: N/A

Booster Involvement Prohibited: N/A

Governance: Legislation

Transfer Inducement Language: N/A

Prohibited Categories: N/A

Policy Updated: May 2021

NEBRASKA

State Athletic Association: Nebraska School Activities Association
Association Website: https://nsaahome.org/
High School NIL Allowed: Yes
Disclosure Required: Yes
Prior Approval Required: No
School Logo Use: Prohibited
Booster Involvement Prohibited: Yes
Governance: Legislation
Transfer Inducement Language: Yes
Prohibited Categories: Yes
Policy Updated: July 2020

NEVADA

State Athletic Association: Nevada Interscholastic Activities Association
Association Website: https://www.niaa.com/
High School NIL Allowed: Yes
Disclosure Required: Yes
Prior Approval Required: No
School Logo Use: Prohibited
Booster Involvement Prohibited: Yes
Governance: Legislation
Transfer Inducement Language: Yes
Prohibited Categories: Yes
Policy Updated: June 2021

NEW HAMPSHIRE
State Athletic Association: New Hampshire Interscholastic Athletic Association
Association Website: https://www.nhiaa.org/
High School NIL Allowed: Yes
Disclosure Required: Yes
Prior Approval Required: Unclear
School Logo Use: Prohibited
Booster Involvement Prohibited: Unclear
Governance: Athletic Association
Transfer Inducement Language: Unclear
Prohibited Categories: Yes
Policy Updated: N/A

NEW JERSEY
State Athletic Association: New Jersey State Interscholastic Athletic Association
Association Website: https://www.njsiaa.org/
High School NIL Allowed: Yes
Disclosure Required: Yes
Prior Approval Required: No
School Logo Use: Prohibited
Booster Involvement Prohibited: Yes
Governance: Legislation
Transfer Inducement Language: Yes
Prohibited Categories: Yes
Policy Updated: September 2020

NEW MEXICO
State Athletic Association: New Mexico Activities Association
Association Website: https://www.nmact.org/
High School NIL Allowed: Yes
Disclosure Required: Yes
Prior Approval Required: No
School Logo Use: Prohibited
Booster Involvement Prohibited: Yes
Governance: Legislation
Transfer Inducement Language: Yes
Prohibited Categories: Yes
Policy Updated: April 2021

NEW YORK
State Athletic Association: New York State Public High School Athletic Association
Association Website: https://nysphsaa.org/
High School NIL Allowed: Yes
Disclosure Required: Yes
Prior Approval Required: No
School Logo Use: Prohibited
Booster Involvement Prohibited: Yes
Governance: Legislation
Transfer Inducement Language: Yes
Prohibited Categories: Yes
Policy Updated: November 2021

NORTH CAROLINA

State Athletic Association: North Carolina High School Athletic Association
Association Website: https://www.nchsaa.org/
High School NIL Allowed: Yes
Disclosure Required: Yes
Prior Approval Required: Yes
School Logo Use: Prohibited
Booster Involvement Prohibited: Yes
Governance: Legislation and Athletic Association
Transfer Inducement Language: Yes
Prohibited Categories: Yes
Policy Updated: July 2021

NORTH DAKOTA

State Athletic Association: North Dakota High School Activities Association
Association Website: https://ndhsaanow.com/
High School NIL Allowed: Yes
Disclosure Required: Yes
Prior Approval Required: Unclear
School Logo Use: Prohibited
Booster Involvement Prohibited: Yes
Governance: Athletic Association
Transfer Inducement Language: Yes
Prohibited Categories: Yes
Policy Updated: N/A

OHIO

State Athletic Association: Ohio High School Athletic Association
Association Website: https://www.ohsaa.org/
High School NIL Allowed: Yes
Disclosure Required: Yes
Prior Approval Required: No
School Logo Use: Prohibited
Booster Involvement Prohibited: Yes
Governance: Athletic Association
Transfer Inducement Language: Yes
Prohibited Categories: Yes
Policy Updated: June 2023

OKLAHOMA

State Athletic Association: Oklahoma Secondary School Activities
Association
Association Website: https://ossaaillustrated.com/
High School NIL Allowed: Yes
Disclosure Required: Yes
Prior Approval Required: No
School Logo Use: Prohibited
Booster Involvement Prohibited: Yes
Governance: Legislation
Transfer Inducement Language: Yes
Prohibited Categories: Yes
Policy Updated: May 2021

OREGON

State Athletic Association: Oregon School Activities Association
Association Website: https://www.osaa.org/
High School NIL Allowed: Yes
Disclosure Required: Yes
Prior Approval Required: No
School Logo Use: Prohibited
Booster Involvement Prohibited: Yes
Governance: Legislation
Transfer Inducement Language: Yes
Prohibited Categories: Yes
Policy Updated: June 2021

PENNSYLVANIA

State Athletic Association: Pennsylvania Interscholastic Athletic Association
Association Website: https://www.piaa.org/
High School NIL Allowed: Yes
Disclosure Required: Yes
Prior Approval Required: No
School Logo Use: Prohibited
Booster Involvement Prohibited: Yes
Governance: Legislation
Transfer Inducement Language: Yes
Prohibited Categories: Yes
Policy Updated: July 2022

RHODE ISLAND

State Athletic Association: Rhode Island Interscholastic League
Association Website: https://www.riil.org/
High School NIL Allowed: Yes
Disclosure Required: Unclear
Prior Approval Required: No
School Logo Use: Prohibited
Booster Involvement Prohibited: Yes
Governance: Athletic Association
Transfer Inducement Language: Yes
Prohibited Categories: Yes
Policy Updated: N/A

SOUTH CAROLINA

State Athletic Association: South Carolina High School League
Association Website: https://schsl.org/
High School NIL Allowed: No
Disclosure Required: N/A
Prior Approval Required: N/A
School Logo Use: N/A
Booster Involvement Prohibited: N/A
Governance: Legislation
Transfer Inducement Language: N/A
Prohibited Categories: N/A
Policy Updated: May 2022

SOUTH DAKOTA

State Athletic Association: South Dakota High School Activities Association

Association Website: https://sdhsaa.com/

High School NIL Allowed: Yes

Disclosure Required: Yes

Prior Approval Required: No

School Logo Use: Prohibited

Booster Involvement Prohibited: Yes

Governance: Athletic Association

Transfer Inducement Language: Yes

Prohibited Categories: Yes

Policy Updated: N/A

TENNESSEE

State Athletic Association: Tennessee Secondary School Athletic Association

Association Website: https://tssaa.org/

High School NIL Allowed: Yes

Disclosure Required: Yes

Prior Approval Required: No

School Logo Use: Prohibited

Booster Involvement Prohibited: Yes

Governance: Legislation

Transfer Inducement Language: Yes

Prohibited Categories: Yes

Policy Updated: May 2022

TEXAS

State Athletic Association: Texas University Interscholastic League
Association Website: https://www.uiltexas.org/
High School NIL Allowed: Yes
Disclosure Required: Yes
Prior Approval Required: No
School Logo Use: Prohibited
Booster Involvement Prohibited: Yes
Governance: Legislation and Athletic Association
Transfer Inducement Language: Yes
Prohibited Categories: Yes
Policy Updated: June 2023
NOTES: 17 and older

UTAH

State Athletic Association: Utah High School Activities Association
Association Website: https://uhsaa.org/
High School NIL Allowed: Yes
Disclosure Required: Yes
Prior Approval Required: No
School Logo Use: Prohibited
Booster Involvement Prohibited: Yes
Governance: Legislation
Transfer Inducement Language: Yes
Prohibited Categories: Yes
Policy Updated: March 2021

VERMONT

State Athletic Association: Vermont Principals Association

Association Website: https://vpaonline.org/

High School NIL Allowed: Yes

Disclosure Required: Yes

Prior Approval Required: No

School Logo Use: Prohibited

Booster Involvement Prohibited: Yes

Governance: Athletic Association

Transfer Inducement Language: Yes

Prohibited Categories: Yes

Policy Updated: N/A

VIRGINIA

State Athletic Association: Virginia High School League

Association Website: https://www.vhsl.org/

High School NIL Allowed: Yes

Disclosure Required: Yes

Prior Approval Required: No

School Logo Use: Prohibited

Booster Involvement Prohibited: Yes

Governance: Legislation

Transfer Inducement Language: Yes

Prohibited Categories: Yes

Policy Updated: April 18, 2024

WASHINGTON
State Athletic Association: Washington Interscholastic Activities
Association
Association Website: https://www.wiaa.com/
High School NIL Allowed: Yes
Disclosure Required: Yes
Prior Approval Required: No
School Logo Use: Prohibited
Booster Involvement Prohibited: Yes
Governance: Legislation
Transfer Inducement Language: Yes
Prohibited Categories: Yes
Policy Updated: May 2021

WEST VIRGINIA
State Athletic Association: West Virginia Secondary School Activities
Commission
Association Website: https://www.wvssac.org/
High School NIL Allowed: Yes
Disclosure Required: Yes
Prior Approval Required: No
School Logo Use: Prohibited
Booster Involvement Prohibited: Yes
Governance: Athletic Association
Transfer Inducement Language: Yes
Prohibited Categories: Yes
Policy Updated: N/A

WISCONSIN

State Athletic Association: Wisconsin Interscholastic Athletic Association
Association Website: https://www.wiaawi.org/
High School NIL Allowed: Yes
Disclosure Required: Yes
Prior Approval Required: No
School Logo Use: Prohibited
Booster Involvement Prohibited: Yes
Governance: Athletic Association
Transfer Inducement Language: Yes
Prohibited Categories: Yes
Policy Updated: N/A

WYOMING

State Athletic Association: Wyoming High School Activities Association
Association Website: https://www.whsaa.org/
High School NIL Allowed: No
Disclosure Required: N/A
Prior Approval Required: N/A
School Logo Use: N/A
Booster Involvement Prohibited: N/A
Governance: Athletic Association
Transfer Inducement Language: N/A
Prohibited Categories: N/A
Policy Updated: N/A

A Calm Framework for the Next Three Years

FILM ROOM

Nolan was a sophomore when his parents first started hearing about NIL.

At a weekend tournament, another parent mentioned that a player from a nearby school had partnered with a local training facility. The arrangement was small, some social media posts and a few appearances at youth camps, but it was enough to spark conversation among the parents watching from the stands.

By the next week, Nolan's father had read several articles online about NIL. Most of them focused on college athletes and the large endorsement deals that occasionally make headlines. The stories were exciting, but they also created a sense that something important might be happening quickly.

After practice one evening, Nolan's father asked him a question that many athletes eventually hear.

"Should we be doing something with NIL right now?"

Nolan shrugged.

He had just finished a two-hour practice, was trying to keep his grades steady, and his team had a difficult stretch of games ahead.

His father's question wasn't unreasonable. Parents want to support their children, and when a new opportunity appears in sports culture, it is natural to wonder whether something important might be happening. But the truth was much simpler, Nolan needed time.

Over the next two seasons, Nolan continued doing what most developing athletes do. He trained, he competed, and he slowly improved. His role on the team expanded. By the beginning of his senior year, he had become one of the most consistent players in the program.

During that final season, a local sporting goods store approached him about promoting a youth clinic they were sponsoring. Just a few social media posts and an appearance at the clinic. Nolan's family handled the situation carefully. They checked the school's policy, disclosed the opportunity to the athletic director, and made sure the promotion did not use school branding or imply a team endorsement.

The clinic went well and the younger athletes enjoyed meeting him. The store gained some visibility in the community. It was a win for everybody. The NIL opportunity was real, but it was also small, local, and appropriate for a high school athlete.

Most importantly, it arrived naturally.

Nolan did not chase it. His family did not try to manufacture it. It grew out of the reputation he had built over several years of steady development.

When parents ask what the next three years should look like, Nolan's story offers a useful reminder. Most athletes do not need a complicated NIL plan. They need a framework that keeps the focus where it belongs.

The Question Parents Eventually Ask

At some point during high school athletics, most families begin asking a similar question. "What should we actually be doing right now?"

By the time parents reach this point, they have often learned quite a bit about the landscape surrounding modern youth sports. They may have heard about NIL opportunities, recruiting timelines, social media expectations, and eligibility rules that vary from state to state.

That information can be helpful, but it can also create a feeling that something important needs to happen quickly. The truth is that the path forward is rarely as complicated as it first appears.

High school athletics still follow the same basic structure they always have. Athletes develop over time, opportunities expand gradually, and the majority of important decisions occur later than families initially expect.

The real challenge for parents is not finding information. It is keeping perspective as information accumulates.

The next three years of an athlete's high school career do not require constant strategic decisions. They require a steady approach built around a few consistent priorities.

Three Priorities That Matter Most

Most high school athletic development revolves around three priorities: development, exposure, and responsibility.

These priorities are easy to overlook because modern sports culture often emphasizes visibility and promotion. Social media platforms reward attention in the form of likes, comments and shares. Recruiting announcements appear constantly online, real or not. NIL headlines can make it seem as though financial opportunity is an immediate possibility for every athlete.

But when coaches evaluate athletes, whether at the high school or college level, they rarely begin with attention. They begin with development. Athletes who improve their skills, compete consistently, and demonstrate maturity over time place themselves in the strongest position for future opportunities. Exposure and recognition tend to follow naturally.

Responsibility is the final element that ties the process together. Athletes who handle attention responsibly, communicate well with coaches, and represent themselves positively within their communities create trust. Development builds ability. Exposure helps people notice that ability. Responsibility builds trust around it.

When those three elements work together, opportunities, whether recruiting opportunities or NIL opportunities, become much easier to navigate.

Freshman and Sophomore Years: Build the Foundation

For most athletes, the early years of high school are primarily about building a foundation.

Athletes are still growing physically and mentally. Coaches are still learning what each player can contribute to a team. Performance can fluctuate from week to week as athletes adapt to the increased demands of high school competition.

During this stage, development matters far more than visibility. Athletes benefit most from focusing on habits that improve long-term performance: consistent training, attention to coaching feedback, and the ability to compete with discipline even when results are inconsistent.

Recruiting conversations are typically limited during these early years. College coaches may observe younger athletes, particularly in sports with early scouting cultures, but firm decisions are rarely made.

The same principle applies to NIL.

In states where high school NIL is permitted, it is possible for younger athletes to participate in modest promotional activities. A local training facility might ask an athlete to post about a youth clinic. A sporting goods store might invite a player to appear at a community event. These opportunities are generally small and local. They should remain secondary to development.

Families sometimes worry that ignoring early NIL opportunities could mean missing something important. In practice, the opposite is usually true. Athletes who build their skills first tend to find that opportunities later become easier to manage.

Junior Year: Opportunities Begin to Expand

By the time athletes reach their junior year, the picture often becomes clearer.

Several seasons of competition have revealed patterns in performance and improvement. Athletes have developed relationships with coaches and teammates. Their physical growth has begun to stabilize, and their role within the team is often better defined. Recruiting conversations frequently become more specific during this period. College coaches who have been observing an athlete may begin communicating more directly.

Exposure also tends to increase during this stage. Athletes may participate in camps, tournaments, or showcases where college programs evaluate talent more closely. NIL opportunities, when they appear for high school athletes, often begin to emerge around this time as well.

Local businesses may notice athletes who have developed a strong reputation within their communities. A training facility may invite a player to promote a clinic. A community business may see value in partnering with an athlete who represents local sports positively.

These arrangements are usually modest in scope. They are rarely life-changing financially, and they are not meant to be. High school NIL works best when it feels like a community partnership rather than a commercial enterprise. When families approach these opportunities with transparency and respect for school policies, they tend to proceed without controversy.

Junior year is also when athletes begin to experience something new: attention. Attention can be exciting, but it also carries responsibility. Social media posts travel further. Conversations with coaches carry greater weight. Public behavior becomes more visible.

Athletes who remain steady during this stage often distinguish themselves in ways that statistics alone cannot capture.

Senior Year: Finish With Perspective

Senior year often arrives more quickly than families expect.

Athletes who have spent several years developing their skills and reputation begin to see the results of that work. Recruiting decisions may become clearer. Future plans begin to take shape. For some athletes, that means continuing their careers in college athletics. For others, it means finishing high school sports with pride and transitioning to new pursuits.

NIL opportunities, when they occur during this stage, should still follow the same principles guided by earlier decisions.

- Is the opportunity transparent?
- Is it independent from team participation?
- Does it respect school and state policies?

When those questions can be answered clearly, most NIL activities remain manageable.

Senior year also presents athletes with a final opportunity to demonstrate maturity. The way an athlete handles success, disappointment, and increased visibility often leaves a lasting impression on coaches and community members.

The Quiet Advantage of Patience

One of the most common challenges facing families is the pressure to move quickly.

Sports culture often rewards urgency. Athletes see recruiting announcements online. They see highlight videos circulating widely. They see stories about NIL deals that appear far larger than anything happening within their own communities.

This environment can make it feel as though something important must happen immediately. But the athletes who navigate high school sports most successfully often share a quieter trait, they remain patient.

They continue developing their skills even when attention fluctuates. They communicate openly with coaches and administrators. They approach opportunities carefully instead of chasing them aggressively.

A Simple Framework

If the landscape surrounding NIL and recruiting ever begins to feel overwhelming, it helps to return to a simple framework.

Focus on development first and maintain responsible behavior both on and off the field. In this way, you allow opportunities to grow naturally from reputation and performance. This approach may not produce dramatic headlines, but it tends to create the healthiest long-term outcomes for athletes and families.

When development and responsibility combine, NIL becomes easier to understand and manage.

Looking Ahead

The landscape of high school athletics will continue evolving. NIL policies will change, technology will influence recruiting in new ways, and athletes will encounter opportunities that previous generations never experienced. But the fundamentals of development and character rarely change.

Athletes who focus on growth, respect the structure of school athletics, and approach opportunities with maturity position themselves well for whatever comes next.

For parents, the most helpful role is often the simplest one. Provide perspective. When families do this consistently, the next three years of high school athletics tend to unfold more smoothly than they first imagined.

And when opportunities arrive, as they sometimes do, athletes are ready to handle them with confidence.

Final Thoughts: Opportunity Without Panic

Youth sports today can make everything feel urgent. Recruiting timelines appear earlier than they once did. Social media highlights the achievements of athletes across the country. Headlines about large NIL deals occasionally create the impression money has suddenly become a central part of high school athletics.

When families first encounter this information, a familiar set of questions tends to follow.

- Are we behind?
- Should we be doing something right now?
- Is everyone else moving faster than we are?

Those reactions are understandable. They come from the same place most decisions in youth sports come from, parents wanting to support their children and give them the best chance to succeed.

But one of the most consistent truths about high school athletics is also one of the most reassuring: Most athletes are not behind; they are simply developing.

The purpose of this book has not been to convince families that NIL is the center of the high school sports experience. If anything, the goal has been the opposite. The goal has been to make NIL understandable enough that it stops feeling mysterious or intimidating.

Once NIL is understood, it becomes easier to place it where it belongs. The landscape surrounding NIL is still evolving. Policies vary by state. School districts continue refining procedures. Athletic associations adjust guidance as they learn from early experiences. That variability can sometimes make the system appear confusing, but it is simply what happens when a new idea is integrated into a long-standing structure.

High school athletics have always been guided by principles that emphasize fairness, education, and competitive balance. As NIL becomes part of that structure, those same principles still apply. Families who understand this tend to approach NIL with a steadier perspective. They do not treat it as a race. They treat it as a system to understand.

For parents, the role has not changed as much as it might seem. Conversations about training, teamwork, academics, and sportsmanship still matter far more than any discussion about endorsements or promotion.

The families who handle NIL best usually approach it the same way they approach everything else in youth sports. They ask questions, they communicate openly with coaches and administrators, and they treat opportunities carefully rather than urgently. Such a mindset allows athletes to grow within the structure of high school sports without feeling pressure to turn their experience into something larger than it needs to be.

Development is still the priority

Athletes improve gradually. Skills sharpen through repetition. Confidence grows through both success and setbacks. Coaches and teammates shape this process in ways that often cannot be measured by statistics or highlight videos.

Development rarely produces headlines, but it is the foundation behind every meaningful opportunity. Athletes who focus on improvement, who listen to coaching, and who support their teammates build something more durable than attention. They build reputation.

The same qualities that have always mattered in sports still matter now.

- Effort.
- Integrity.
- Consistency.

One of the most useful perspectives families can adopt is learning to separate opportunity from urgency. Opportunity is healthy. It reflects recognition of an athlete's work and growth. Urgency, however, can distort judgment. When families feel rushed, they may accept arrangements before fully understanding them. They may react to announcements or headlines instead of focusing on what is actually happening within their own program.

The athletes who navigate recruiting and NIL most successfully usually avoid this sense of urgency. They understand that meaningful opportunities rarely disappear overnight. Coaches respect families who communicate openly and thoughtfully. Businesses interested in partnerships tend to value authenticity more than speed.

It Takes a Village

It is important to remember that high school athletics exist within communities. Coaches, teachers, administrators, teammates, and families all shape the experience of young athletes. NIL does not replace those relationships. When approached thoughtfully, it can even strengthen them. Local businesses often support athletes because they believe in the positive role sports play in their communities. Younger athletes look up to older players who demonstrate leadership and maturity.

In that context, NIL becomes less about promotion and more about representation.

For most athletes, high school sports eventually come to an end. Some will continue competing in college. Many will move on to entirely different paths. But the lessons learned through sports tend to remain. Athletes remember teammates who pushed them to improve and coaches who believed in their potential. They also remember the satisfaction that comes from steady progress. Those experiences form a foundation that extends far beyond the playing field.

NIL, when it appears, becomes only a small part of that larger journey. It may offer lessons in responsibility, communication, and decision-making. But it rarely defines the experience. Development and growth do. Growth as an athlete, and more importantly, growth as a person.

Continuing the Conversation

The landscape surrounding high school NIL will continue to evolve. Policies will change. Schools and athletic associations will refine their guidance. New questions will appear as athletes, families, and communities gain more experience with the system.

Because of that, staying informed can be helpful.

Families who want updates, practical guidance, and additional resources related to high school NIL can visit ProspectBridgeSports.com, where educational materials and updates about the changing NIL landscape will continue to be shared.

The goal is not to create urgency. It is simply to provide clear information so families can make thoughtful decisions as the environment continues to develop.

In the end, most high school athletic careers will not be defined by NIL deals or recruiting rankings. They will be defined by the quieter parts of the experience, early practices, long bus rides, teammates who become lifelong friends, and the pride that comes from steady improvement.

Name, image, and likeness opportunities may appear along the way. When they do, families who understand the system can approach them calmly and responsibly.

But the lasting value of high school sports has always been something deeper. It is the opportunity to grow.

If athletes focus on that growth, enjoy competing with their teammates, and carry themselves with integrity, they will leave the game with something far more meaningful than any short-term opportunity. They will leave with lessons that last long after the final season ends.